BERNAR
CLAIRV

Other HarperCollins Spiritual Classics:

BERNARD OF CLAIRVAUX

Selected Works

Foreword by Vinita Hampton Wright

Edited by Emilie Griffin

Translation by G. R. Evans

HarperOne

An Imprint of HarperCollinsPublishers

HarperOne

BERNARD OF CLAIRVAUX: *Selected Works*. Original translation by Paulist Press, 997 Macarthur Boulevard, Mahwah, NJ 07430; www.paulistpress.com. Copyright © 1987 by Gillian R. Evans. Foreword © 2005 by Vinita Hampton Wright. All rights reserved. Printed in the United States of America. No part of this book may be used or reproduced in any manner whatsoever without written permission except in the case of brief quotations embodied in critical articles and reviews. For information address HarperCollins Publishers, 195 Broadway, New York, NY 10007.

HarperCollins books may be purchased for educational, business, or sales promotional use. For information, please e-mail the Special Markets Department at SPsales@harpercollins.com.

HarperCollins website: http://www.harpercollins.com
HarperCollins®, ♥®, and HarperOne™ are trademarks of HarperCollins Publishers.

Library of Congress Cataloging-in-Publication Data
Bernard, or Clairvaux, Saint, 1090 or 91–1153
    [Selections. English. 2005]
    Bernard of Clairvaux : selected works / edited by Emilie Griffin ; translation by G. R. Evans ; foreword by Vinita Hampton Wright.
        p. cm.
    Contents: On conversation—On loving God—Sermons on The song of songs—Selections from his letters.
    ISBN 978-0-06-075067-1
    1. Spiritual life—Catholic Church.   2. Bible. O.T. Song of Solomon—Sermons.
3. Catholic Church—Sermons.   4. Sermons, Latin—Translations into English.   I. Title: Selected works.   II. Griffin, Emilie.   III. Evans, G. R. (Gillian Rosemary)   IV. Title.

BX2349.B39213   2005
248.4'82—dc22   2005045956

HB 10.20.2020

CONTENTS

FOREWORD

*"Our true life is to be found only through conversion, and there is no
other way to enter upon it."*

I did not grow up paying attention to the saints. My mother's
people were Assemblies of God, and my father's mother took me
to the Methodist church when I was a child. At that little church,
tucked away in Kansas farmland, a Pentecostal evangelist preached
a revival when I was about eleven, and I experienced what I can
only call a conversion. I wept at the altar rail, unable to put into
words the shift that I sensed happening at the bottom of myself. I
simply knew that I wanted to follow Jesus. A year or so later, my
4-H club visited a Baptist mission church down the street from
my house. On that Sunday morning, an unpretentious man
opened a Bible and read from it and then proceeded to preach
from it. Another shift occurred, something I later identified as my
heart burning within me, to use a phrase coined by those two
disciples on the road to Emmaus who resonated so powerfully
with the words Jesus had spoken to them. I recognized in the
Bible something for which my soul hungered. After that 4-H
Sunday, I walked the four blocks every week to worship with the
Baptists, and I was baptized there at age thirteen.

I was officially a member of the Southern Baptist denomina-
tion through high school and college and did not officially break
from it until grad school at age thirty. By then my soul had gone
through yet more revolutions, having followed its longing for
liturgy, ritual, and mystery, which are foreign in many evangelical

traditions and which were downright suspect in the ones that had nurtured my early life. Even then, I had little use for saints, because my studies did not take me that direction and I still harbored a vague fear that close association with dead Christians would lead straight to idolatry.

By age forty I was worshipping with Catholics and by forty-two was working for a Catholic book publisher. Turn, turn went the soul, opening a little more here, navigating new vocabulary there. Within a few years I had edited books about the saints and had begun to be more hospitable toward them.

Now, at age forty-seven, I am an Episcopalian, having not fallen far from the Anglican tree that was likely my paternal grandmother's tradition, or at least the tradition of her forebears back in England. And I am happy that my worship includes regular remembrance of the saints. The passing years and the artistic life have taught me that past, present, and future are realities only so long as I dwell on this globe that whirls around a star. The communion of saints is ever present, connecting me to the universe in ways that ordinary mortals cannot. They are integral to what holds the decades and generations together in some comprehensible order.

As I read what Bernard of Clairvaux wrote about conversion, I sense that this saint has been connected to me all my life, even when I did not know him. He has likely watched the turns of my every conversion, and, although he lived in the twelfth century, he understood that journey as well as any present-day psychologist. I'm amazed at what he was able to articulate about processes of the soul. As a writer, an editor, and a facilitator of workshops about creativity and spirituality, I have discovered a lot about process. I have come to respect that the soul has its ways of leading us to growth, truth, and healing, something that dear Bernard figured out centuries ago. Whether he is talking about conversion to faith or the attainment of love, he carefully arranges the idea and helps us see how we proceed from one level to the next of knowing God and ourselves.

Bernard spent his life writing, teaching, and talking, trying to make the words fall right so that heretics would see their error, so that believers would not lose heart but instead keep moving forward in their faith, and so that lovers of God would learn how to live out their love with authenticity and passion:

> Neither fear nor love of self can convert the soul. They change the appearance of one's deeds from time to time, but never one's character.

When I was in my twenties, I wrote a little essay, "The ABCs of Delight," about how a person comes to delight in God. I don't know if the piece is still in my files; it probably was tedious and not very good. But as I read some of Bernard's material about loving God, I remembered my own struggles, for the past three decades, to articulate the soul's pilgrimage toward God. I write and edit for a living now, and the only reason I can, in good conscience, keep adding to the mountain of books out there is that, from time to time, we do get the words right, and those words do make a difference in the world. When I read Bernard's prose— his urgency for people to care about their souls, his patience in lining out the concepts—I feel the weight and the glory of my responsibility to be a wordsmith in this, an age far removed from Bernard's world.

His living and effective word is a kiss; not a meeting of lips, which can sometimes be deceptive about the state of the heart, but a full infusion of joys, a revelation of secrets, a wonderful and inseparable mingling of the light from above and the mind on which it is shed, which, when it is joined with God, is one spirit with him.

It's impressive that someone like Bernard of Clairvaux dared to take on a subject like the Song of Songs. He was a vowed celibate, and his culture was not at all comfortable with sex. Nevertheless, he went straight to the heart of what it means to be in love, to ache with desire for another, and he used those natural yearnings to bring God close to us in a stunning fashion. It's as simple as this: God is our lover. All our desire is unfulfilled until it is filled by divine love, and that filling goes beyond any other form of satisfaction.

One of my chief frustrations about creative work in the American landscape is how it has been crippled by a warped understanding of sexuality. We waver constantly between repression and fear of sex and the sheer worship and mutilation of it. The more I work as an artist, the more evident it becomes to me that sexuality and spirituality arise from a common passion, and each informs the other as the person proceeds toward integrity of body and soul. And so I am quite grateful that Bernard allowed, all those years ago, for sexuality to be a teacher about spirituality.

Like so many others, he could have avoided sexuality altogether and demonized it. Instead he discerned its proper location in the life of a person who is moving toward unity with a loving God:

> These are the Lord's words. You cannot disbelieve them. Let them believe what they do not know from experience, so that by their faith they may in the future have the reward of experience.

Bernard is one of the people in this universe who hold on to faith that I do not yet possess, and perhaps this is one of the most crucial roles of a saint. He has journeyed farther toward God than I have, and he assures me that if I simply keep moving and following my longing after Divine Love, I will in fact arrive at it for real. This is help and hope that I cannot live without.

—VINITA HAMPTON WRIGHT

ON CONVERSION

Bernard's sermon "On Conversion" was given in 1140 in Paris as a public discourse. It is unique among his sermons in the audience to which it is addressed and also in its point of departure. Bernard is not, for once, preaching to the converted, to those who are trying with all their might to make progress on the road to the presence of God. He is speaking to those who have not yet set out, or at least not purposefully. The term "conversion" at this date had, most commonly, the sense of "deciding to enter a religious order"; but for Bernard it is also conversion of the heart.

He spoke perhaps in the cloister of Notre Dame, to an audience of scholars and students from the schools of Paris: Notre Dame, St. Genevieve, and perhaps St. Victor. His biographer, Geoffrey, and Peter Lombard were in the audience (both were at one time pupils of Hugh of St. Victor). More than twenty of those who heard him were converted. They declared their intention of following him to Clairvaux. He took them to the abbey of St. Denis for the night, and when the next morning they returned to Paris three more joined them. Their conversions were to prove lasting. They were all professed at Clairvaux a year later.

—G. R. Evans

That no one can be converted to the Lord unless the Lord wills it first and calls him with an inner voice

You have come, I believe, to hear the Word of God. I can see no other reason why you should rush here like this! I approve of this desire with all my heart, and I rejoice with you in your praiseworthy zeal. For blessed are those who hear the Word of God—if, that is, they keep it. Blessed are those who are mindful of his laws, provided that they obey them [Ps. 103:18]. Such a one has the words of eternal life indeed, and the hour comes—would it were here now!—when the dead shall hear his voice and they who hear it shall live. For "To do his will is to live" [Ps. 30:5].

And if you would like to know what his will is: It is that we should be converted. Hear what he himself says. "It is not my will that the wicked should perish," says the Lord, "but rather that they should turn from their wickedness and live" [Ezek. 18:23].

From these words we see clearly that our true life is to be found only through conversion, and there is no other way to enter upon it. As the same Lord says, "Unless you are converted and become like little children, you will not enter the kingdom of heaven" [Matt. 18:3]. Truly, only little children will enter, for it is a little child who leads them, he who was born and given to us for this very end. I seek, then, the voice the dead will hear and, when they hear it, live. Perhaps it is even necessary to preach the Gospel to the dead [1 Pet. 4:6].

And meanwhile a word comes to mind, brief but full of meaning, which the mouth of the Lord has spoken, as the prophet bears witness. "You have said," he cries, undoubtedly speaking to the

Lord his God, "be converted, sons of men" [Isa. 1:20; 40:5; Ps. 90:3]. It seems wholly fitting that it is conversion that is required of the sons of men; it is absolutely necessary for sinners. The heavenly spirits are told to give praise, as the same prophet says in the Psalms, "Praise your God, O Zion" [Ps. 147:12]; that is more appropriate for the righteous [Ps. 33:1].

As to the remainder of what he says, "You have said" [Ps. 90:3], I do not think that is to be passed over carelessly or heard unreflectively. For who dare compare the sayings of men with what God is said to have said? The Word of God is living and effective. His voice is a voice of magnificence and power. "He spoke and they were made" [Ps. 148:5]. He said, "Let there be light, and there was light" [Gen. 1:3]. He said, "Be converted" [Ps. 90:3], and the sons of men have been converted. So the conversion of souls is clearly the work of the divine voice, not of any human voice. Even Simon son of John, called and appointed by the Lord to be a fisher of men, will toil in vain all night and catch nothing until he casts his net at the Lord's word. Then he can catch a vast multitude [John 21:15ff; Matt. 4:19].

Would that we too might cast our net at this word today and experience what is written, "Behold he will give his voice the sound of power" [Ps. 68:33]. If I lie, that is my own fault. It will perhaps be judged to be my own voice and not the voice of the Lord if I seek what is my own and not what is Jesus Christ's. For the rest, even if I speak of the righteousness of God and seek God's glory, I can hope that what I say will be effective only if he makes it so. I must ask him to make this voice of mine a voice of power.

I admonish you, therefore, to lift up the ears of your heart to hear this inner voice, so that you may strive to hear inwardly what is said to the outward man. For this is the voice of magnificence and power, rolling through the desert, revealing secrets, shaking souls free of sluggishness [Ps. 29].

That the voice of the Lord speaks and makes itself heard to all, and presents itself even to the soul that does not want to hear

There is no need to make an effort to hear this voice. The difficulty is to shut your ears to it. The voice speaks up; it makes itself heard; it does not cease to knock on everyone's door [Rev. 3:20]. "Forty years long," he says, "I was with this generation, and I said, 'They err constantly in their hearts'" [Ps. 95:10]. He is still with us. He still speaks, even if no one listens. He still says, "They err in their hearts"; Wisdom still cries in the streets. "Come to your senses, evildoers" [Isa. 46:8].

This is the beginning of God's speaking. And this word, which is addressed to all those who are converted in heart, seems to have run on ahead; it is a word that not only calls them back but leads them back and brings them face-to-face with themselves. For it is not so much a voice of power as a ray of light, telling men about their sins and at the same time revealing the things hidden in darkness. There is no difference between this inner voice and light, for they are one and the same Son of God and Word of the Father and brightness of glory.

So too the substance of the soul would seem to be spiritual and simple in its way, without any distinction of senses; the whole soul seems to see and hear at once, if we can speak of it in that way. For what is the purpose of the ray of light or the Word but to bring man to know himself? Indeed, the book of conscience is opened, the wretched passage of life up to now recalled to mind; the sad story is told again; reason is enlightened and what is in the memory is unfolded as though set out before each man's eyes. But reason and memory are not so much "of" the soul as themselves the soul, so that it is both gazer and what is gazed upon, brought face-to-face with itself and overcome by the force of its realization of what it is seeing. It judges itself in its own court. Who can bear this judgment without pain? "My soul is troubled within me" [Ps. 42:6], says the prophet of the Lord, and do you wonder that you cannot be brought to face yourself without being aware of sin, without disturbance, without confusion?

How by this means the soul's reason can judge and discern how to point to all its own evils and criticize them, as if they were written in a book

Do not hope to hear from me what reason seizes on in your memory to blame, what it judges, what it discerns. Listen to the inner voice; use the eyes of your heart, and you will learn by experience. "For no one knows what is in a man except the spirit that is within him" [1 Cor. 2:11]. If pride, envy, greed, ambition, or any other vice is hidden, it can scarcely escape this examination. If there is fornication, rape, cruelty, deception, or any fault at all, it will not be hidden from this judge who is himself the guilty party; nor will it be denied in his presence.

For however quickly all the prurience of delighting in iniquity passed, and however briefly the enticements of pleasure were attractive, the memory is left with a bitter impression, and dirty footprints remain. Into that repository as if into some cesspit runs all abomination and uncleanness. It is a big book in which everything is written with the pen of truth. The stomach endures that bitterness now [Rev. 10:9–10]. Although as it was swallowed it gave a passing pleasure to the taste, that was soon forgotten. I grieve for my stomach; I grieve for it. Why should I not grieve for the stomach of my memory, which is congested with such foulness?

My brothers, which of us, if he suddenly noticed that the clothing covering him was spattered all over with filth and the foulest mud, would not be violently disgusted, quickly take it off, and cast it from him indignantly? But the soul that finds itself contaminated in this way cannot cast itself away as a man can cast away his clothes. Which of us is so patient and so brave that if he were to see his own flesh suddenly shining white with leprosy (as we read happened to Moses's sister Mary), he could stand calmly and thank his Creator [Num. 12:10]? But what is that flesh but the corruptible garment in which we are clothed?

And how should we think of this leprosy of the body in all the elect but as a rod of fatherly correction and a purgation of the heart? It is a great tribulation and a most just cause of sorrow when a man who has been woken from the sleep of wretched pleasure begins to perceive his inward leprosy, which he has brought upon himself with much zeal and effort. No one hates his own flesh. Much less can the soul hate itself.

That he who loves wickedness is shown to hate not only his soul but also his flesh

Perhaps this text in the Psalms strikes one of you: "He who loves wickedness hates his own soul" [Ps. 11:5]. But I say he hates his body too. Surely he hates what he is saving up day by day for hell, what by his hardness and impenitence of heart he is treasuring up for the day of wrath? For this hatred of body and soul is not so much found in the form of a feeling; rather, it is revealed by its effects. Thus the madman hates his body when he lays hands on himself when his powers of rational thought are asleep. But is any madness worse than impenitence of heart and an obstinate will to sin? If a man lays wicked hands on himself, it is not his flesh but his mind that he tears and damages. If you have seen a man tearing at his hands and rubbing them together until they bleed, you have a clear image in him of the sinner's soul. Pleasure turns to pain and agony follows itching. While the man was scratching, he ignored the consequences, although he knew what would happen.

In the same way we have lacerated ourselves and given ourselves ulcers on our unhappy souls with our own hands—except that in a spiritual creature it is more serious because its nature is finer, and so more difficult to mend. We have not done it in a spirit of enmity, but in a stupor of inner insensibility. The absent mind does not notice the internal damage, for it is not looking inward, but perhaps concentrating on its stomach—or beneath the stomach. The minds of some men are on their plates, of others in their pockets. "Where your treasure is," he says, "there is your heart" [Matt. 6:21]. Is it surprising if a soul does not feel its wound when it is not noticing what is happening to it and is somewhere else far away? The time will come when it will return to itself and realize how cruelly it has eviscerated itself in its wretched pursuit. For it could not feel that while it was like a filthy spider weaving a web out of its own body with insatiable greed to catch its vile booty of flies.

Of the punishment of soul and body after death and of the fruitlessness of repentance

But this return will undoubtedly be after death, when all the gates of the body by which the soul has been used to wandering off to busy itself in useless pursuits and going out to seek the passing things of this world will be shut, and it will be forced to remain within itself; for it will have no means of escaping from itself. Truly that will be a most dreadful return and eternal wretchedness, when it can no longer repent or do penance. For where there is no body, there is no possibility of action. Where there is no action, no satisfaction can be made. Thus to repent is to grieve; to do penance is a remedy for sorrow. He who has no hands cannot lift his heart in his hands to heaven. He who has not come to himself before the death of the flesh must remain trapped in himself for eternity.

But in what a self? Whatever he has made himself in this life, such he will be found when he leaves this life, or perhaps even worse, for he will never be better. For he has himself. Now he lays down his body; now he receives it back again, yet not to penance but to punishment, where the state of sin and flesh will be seen to be so much alike that, however our body is punished, its sin can never be expiated and the body's torment can never be ended nor the body killed by torture. Truly, indeed, vengeance rages forever, for it can never wipe out sin. Nor can the body's substance be worn away, for then the affliction of the flesh would come to an end. He who fears this, let him beware, brothers; for he who does not take care will fall into it.

In the present we must feel and throttle the worm of conscience, rather than nurturing it and thus nourishing it for eternity.

To come back to that voice we were speaking of, it is good that we should come to our senses while "the way is open by which he shows us his salvation" [Ps. 50:23], he who with such zealous love calls back those who have strayed.

Let us not meanwhile resent the gnawing of that worm within. Nor let a dangerous tenderness of mind or pernicious softness persuade us that we want to hide our present trouble. It is far better for it to gnaw now, when it can be destroyed by gnawing itself to death. For now, let it gnaw at the putrid stuff, so that it may consume it by its gnawing, and be itself consumed, and in that way it will not begin to be cherished into immortality. "Their worm," it says, "does not die and its fire is not extinguished" [Isa. 66:24]. Who will endure the gnawing?

For now a manifold consolation eases the torture of the accusing conscience. God is kind and does not allow us to be tempted beyond what we can bear or let the worm do us too much harm. Especially at the beginning of our conversion, he anoints our ulcers with the oil of mercy, so that we may not be too much aware of the seriousness of our illness or the difficulty of curing it. In fact, the ease of his healing seems to smile on the penitent. But after a time, that vanishes, when his senses have been trained and the battle is given into his own hands for him to win and learn that Wisdom is stronger than all things. In the meanwhile, he who has heard the voice of the Lord, "Come to your senses, evildoers" [Isa. 46:8], and who has discovered the wickednesses in the depth of his heart, is eager to root them out one by one and curious to find out how each of them got there. The entrance—or rather the entrances—are not hard to find if you look. But no little grief comes from his examination, for he finds that death came in through his own windows [Jer. 9:21]. It becomes clear that the roving eyes, the itching ears, the pleasures of smelling, tasting, and touching have let in many of them. For the spiritual vices we were speaking of are still difficult for the fleshly man to see. That is why he perceives less clearly or not at all those that are the more serious, and his conscience is not troubled as much by the memory of pride or envy as by the recollection of shameful or wicked deeds.

How it seems to some that the human will can easily obey the divine word

And behold a voice from heaven saying, "Be still, you have sinned." And this is what it says. An overflowing sewer now contaminates the whole house with intolerable filth. It is vain for you to empty it when the filth is still flooding in, to repent while you do not cease to sin. For who approves of the fasting of those who fast for strife and contention and smite with the fist of wickedness, but indulge themselves and do as they please? "This is not the fast that I have chosen," says the Lord [Isa. 58:6]. Close the windows, fasten the doors, block all entry carefully, and when at last you are not contending with the entry of fresh filth, you will be able to clean up what is already there. If a man thinks that what he is asked to do is easy, it is as though he did not know about spiritual warfare. For who can say that I do not know how to govern my own members? So fasting puts an end to gluttony and forbids drunkenness; the ears are stopped up to prevent them hearing of blood, the eyes turned from vanity; the hand is directed not to acquisitiveness but to almsgiving and put to work to stop its thieving, as it is written, "He who was a thief is a thief no more; instead, he works with his hands to do good, so that he may have something to give to the needy" [Eph. 4:28].

At this speech the wretch grows pale and is struck dumb with confusion. For his spirit is troubled within him. But the members come to their unhappy mistress without delay to complain bitterly against their master and bewail his hard commands. The greedy sense of taste complains at the meanness of the limit set to it and the forbidding of the pleasure of gluttony. The eye complains that it is told to weep and not wander. While these complaints are going on, the will, stirred up and fiercely angry, says, "Are you telling me a dream or a story?" Now the tongue, which has discovered its own cause for complaint, says, "It is all as you have heard. For I too have been ordered not to tell stories or lies and speak henceforth nothing but what is serious and necessary."

While he promulgates laws and makes decrees in this way for

his own members, they suddenly interrupt the voice that is giving them orders and cry with a single impulse, "Where does this new religion come from? It is easy for you to give orders as you like. But someone will be found who will oppose them, who will make new laws to contradict them." "Who is she?" he asks. They answer, "It is someone who is lying at home paralyzed and deeply tormented."

How the will of man resists the divine voice by gluttony, curiosity, pride, and all the fleshly senses

Then the little old woman jumps up furiously, forgetting all her weariness. With hair standing on end, her clothes torn, her breast bared, scratching at her ulcers, grinding her teeth, dry-mouthed, infecting the air with her foul breath, she asks why reason (if any reason remains) is not ashamed to attack and invade the wretched will. "Is this your conjugal faithfulness?" she demands. "Is this the way you feel compassion for me in my suffering? Up to now you have spared me and not added to the pain of my wounds. Perhaps it seemed to you that something ought to be subtracted from my large dowry? But when you have taken this away, what is left? You have merely added to the wretchedness of this weary creature; and you know how once you respected all my wishes.

"But now, would that the threefold malignity of this dreadful sickness under which I labor had fallen on you not me. I am voluptuous. I am curious. I am ambitious. There is no part of me that is free from this threefold ulcer, from the soles of my feet to the top of my head. My gullet and the shameful parts of my body are given up to pleasure; we must name them afresh, one by one. The wandering foot and the undisciplined eye are slaves to curiosity. Ear and tongue serve vanity, while the sinner's oil pours in to make my head greasy. With my tongue I myself supply whatever others seem to have omitted in my praise. I am greatly pleased both to receive praise from others and, when I conveniently can, to praise myself to others, for I always like to be talked about, whether by myself or by others.

"To this sickness your great skill is also in the habit of applying many dressings. Then my very hands, straying everywhere, have no particular task, but now they show themselves to be wholly enslaved to vanity, now to curiosity, now to pleasure. Even so, not all, nor even one of these, has ever been able to satisfy me, for the eye is not satisfied by what it sees, nor the ear by what it hears. But would that sometimes the body were all eye or the members all turned into a gullet to eat with. Then indeed I might have that little consolation that, despite my begging, you are trying to take away from me." So she spoke, and backing away in indignation and fury, she said, "I shall hang on; I shall hang on for a long time."

Reason, now at last stirred to anger, answers back and is not easily confounded

Now the reason understands its vexation. Now it realizes something of the difficulty of what it has undertaken, and the ease with which it thought to proceed seems an illusion. It sees that the memory is full of filth. It sees more and more filth freely pouring into it. It sees the windows open to death and cannot close them, because the will is still weak, although she is yet in command; and from her ulcers a mass of bloody pus is flowing everywhere. Worst of all, the soul sees itself contaminated not by someone else, but by its own body, which is no other than itself. For the soul is so constituted that just as it is the memory that is befouled, so it is the will that destroys. For the soul itself is nothing but reason, memory, and will. But now reason is found to be blind, for it did not see all this until now, and weak, for it cannot repair what it recognizes; the memory is found to be foul and fetid; and the will weak and covered in itching sores. And, to omit nothing that belongs to the man, his very body rebels and every single member is a window through which death enters the soul and ceaselessly makes the confusion worse.

The breath of consolation when the soul hears of the promised happiness of the kingdom of heaven

When it is in this state, let the soul hear the divine voice; in wonder and amazement let it hear him saying, "Blessed are the poor in spirit, for theirs is the kingdom of heaven" [Matt. 5:3]. Who is poorer in spirit than he who in the whole of his own spirit finds no rest, nowhere to lay his head [Matt. 8:20]? Here too is holy advice, that he who displeases himself pleases God, and he who hates his own house, a house full of filth and unhappiness, is invited into the house of glory, a house not made with hands, which will be everlasting in the heavens. It is not surprising if he trembles at the greatness of his condescension, if he finds it hard to believe what he has heard, if, struck with astonishment, he cries, "Does wretchedness then make a man happy?"

If you are in that state, have faith. It is not wretchedness but mercy that makes a man happy, so that humiliation turns to humility and need to strength. "You shall set aside for your inheritance a generous rain, O God; it was failing, but you have made it perfect" [Ps. 68:9]. That weakness is a benefit that seeks the help of a physician, and he who faints does so to his salvation when God perfects him.

That he in whose flesh sin still reigns cannot hope for this kingdom, and so we must note what follows: "Blessed are the meek"

But because there is no way to the kingdom of God without the firstfruits of the kingdom, and he to whom it is not given to rule his own members cannot hope for the kingdom of heaven, there follows, "Blessed are the meek, for they will inherit the earth" [Matt. 5:5]. To put it more plainly, "Check the wild motions of the will and take care to tame the wild beast. You are in bonds. Strive to untie what you can never break. The will is your Eve. You will not prevail against her by using force."

There is no delay. The man, breathing again at these words and thinking again that his task is not impossible, shamefacedly approaches the angry viper and tries to quell it. He speaks of the temptations of the flesh and denounces worldly consolations as vanities, trivial and worthless, short-lived and most dangerous to all who love them.

How to make an end of the goings in and out of lust and gluttony, and the vanity of curiosity and the love of riches

"For this reason," he says, "call yourself a wicked and unprofitable servant" [Matt. 25:30; Luke 19:22]. You cannot deny that you have never been able to satisfy all these demands, even moderately. The pleasures of the throat, which are so highly regarded today, take up scarcely two fingers' breadth; and the small enjoyment of that little fragment is prepared with such trouble and gives rise to such anxiety! By this the upper and lower parts of the body are enlarged, and the swelling stomach is not so much fattened as made pregnant with destruction; and when the bones cannot bear the weight of the flesh, various diseases follow.

With what labor and expense (sometimes of good reputation and honor), even at what danger to life, is the seductive whirlpool of lust stirred, so that the sulfurous vapor, though it glows very little, may drive its maddened victims with goads and treat their intoxicated hearts like bees, which first pour out honey and then sting. This is the man whose heart is torn, whose desires full of anxiety and regret, whose acts of abomination and ignominy, whose fate of remorse and shame are fully recognized at last for what they are.

What do these vain spectacles benefit the body or seem to confer on the soul? For you will find no third part of man that might benefit from curiosity. Frivolous, vain, and empty is that consolation, and I do not know what harder lot I could solicit for him than that he should always have what he wants, he who, when fleeing sweet peace, delights in restless curiosity. It is quite clear that only the passing of all these "delights" is a joy. Besides, it is obvious from its very name that the "vanity of vanities" is nothing [Eccl. 1:2]. Vain indeed is the labor that is carried out from zeal for vanity. "O glory, glory," says the wise man, "among the thousands of mortals, you are nothing but a vain puffing up of the ears!" And yet how much unhappiness do you think this (which is not so much happy vanity as vain happiness) produces? For it causes blindness of heart, as it is written, "My people, those who call you blessed deceive you" [Isa. 3:12]. It produces the stiff-necked fury of animosity, the anxious labor of suspicion, the cruel torment of frustration, and the wretchedness of envy, which receives more misery than pity.

Thus the insatiable love of riches is a desire that brings far more torment to the soul than their enjoyment brings refreshment. For the acquisition of riches is found to be all labor, their possession all fear, and their loss all sorrow. Then, "Where there are many riches, there are many who consume them" [Eccl. 5:10], and indeed other people's use of their riches leaves the rich only the reputation for wealth and the cares of wealth. And in all this for so slight a thing, or not even that—for nothing. To think nothing of the glory that the eye has not seen nor the ear heard, nor has it entered the heart of man, the glory that God has prepared for those who love him, seems to be not so much lack of sense as lack of faith.

On unworthy slavery to the vices, the uncertainty when death will come, and the unhappiness of amassing riches

Surely it is their own fault that this world, which lies in the Evil One's grip, deludes with vain promises souls who forget their creation and their dignity, souls who are not ashamed to feed swine, to keep company with swine in their desires, and not even then to be satisfied with their disgusting food? From this comes such infirmity of purpose and wretched abjection that this noble creature is not ashamed to live in slavery to this foulness of the body's senses, although he is capable of enjoying eternal blessedness and the glory of God's greatness. God created him by his own breath, distinguished him by making him in his own likeness, redeemed him by his blood, gave him faith, adopted him by the Spirit. When the soul deserts such a Bridegroom and pursues such lovers [Hos. 2:7], it is not surprising that it cannot grasp the glory that is prepared for it. It is fitting that it should hunger for husks and not be given them, when it preferred to feed pigs rather than feast at the Father's table [Luke 15:16]. It is the work of madness to feed what is barren and brings forth nothing, to be unwilling to give anything to the widow, to care nothing for the heart and to give the flesh everything it wants, to fatten and caress a putrid body that is destined before long to be the food of worms. For who is unaware that to worship mammon, to serve avarice (which means serving idols), or to chase eagerly after vanity is clear evidence of a degenerate soul?

That works done in this life are like the seeds of everlasting reward

Granted that the world seems for now to give those who love it great and honorable things; everyone knows that it is faithless. Certainly these things do not last and it is uncertain even when they will end. Often they are lost to a man while he is still alive. He is sure to lose them when he dies.

And what in human life is more certain than death and more uncertain than the hour of death? Death is not merciful to poverty. It is no respecter of riches. It spares no one for the sake of his noble birth, his behavior, even his age; it waits at the door for the old and ambushes the young. Unhappy is he who in the dark and slippery places of this life gives his energies to work that cannot last and does not recognize that it is vapor that appears for a moment and vanity of vanities. Ambitious man, have you obtained some dignity you have long desired? Hold on to what you have. Miser, have you filled your coffers? Be careful not to lose it all. Has your land been very fruitful? Pull down your barns and build greater. Make square buildings round. Say to your soul, "You must have goods laid up for many years." There will be someone to say, "Fool, this night your soul will be required of you. To whom will all that you have stored up belong?" [Luke 12:18ff].

And would that only this collection perished and not their collector too! He will perish more terribly. It would be better to sweat over work that has no purpose than at work that has a deadly result. But here the wages of sin is death, and he who sows in the flesh will reap corruption from the flesh. For our deeds do not pass away as they seem to. On the contrary, every deed done in this life is the seed of a harvest to be reaped in eternity. The fool will be amazed when he sees the huge yield of the few seeds he has sown, good or bad, according to the quality of the seed. He who bears this in mind will never think sin a trifle, because he will look to the future harvest rather than what he sows. Men sow unknowingly; they sow, hiding the mysteries of iniquity, and disguise the notes of vanity; the business of darkness is done in the dark.

That it is impossible for the sinner to hide

"I am surrounded by walls," says the man. "Who can see me?" [Sir. 23:18]. Even if no man sees you, you are seen. The wicked angel sees you. The good angel sees you. God, who is greater than good or wicked angels, sees you. The accuser sees you. The multitude of witnesses see you. The Judge himself sees you, before whom you must stand trial, on whose gaze it is madness to turn your back. It is terrible to fall into the hands of the living God.

Do not be in a hurry to think yourself safe. Ambushes are concealed from you, but you cannot hide from them. Ambushes are concealed, I say, and just as you cannot find them, so you cannot fail to fall into them. He who made the ear hears, and he who put the eyes in your head sees. No wall of stones cuts off the Sun's rays.

Not even the wall of the body is impenetrable to the gaze of truth. He sees those he has made. All things lie bare to his eyes, which penetrate more easily than a two-edged sword [Heb. 4:12]. He not only sees; he distinguishes the paths of our thoughts and the sources of our feelings. If he did not see into the uttermost depths of the human heart and perceive what lies in it better than it does itself, man would not fear the sentence of the Lord his judge so much, even when he is not aware of anything that can be held against him. The apostle says, "I know of nothing against myself. But I am not therefore justified. It is the Lord who judges me" [1 Cor. 4:3ff.].

If you boast that you can frustrate human judgment by pretense, be sure that he whose eye is on men even for sins they have not committed will not overlook the sins they do commit. If you stand in such fear of your neighbor's knowledge of what you are, how much less should you shrug off the opinion of those to whom iniquity is the more hateful and corruption far more execrable? If you do not fear God but only the eyes of men, remember what you cannot fail to know, that the man Christ knows all the deeds of men. So, then, what you would scarcely dare before men you should be the more reluctant to dare before him. What you would not, I do not say, be allowed to do, but like to do, while your fellow servant is watching you should be horrified even to think of doing in the presence of your Lord. Otherwise, if you live in fear of the eye of the flesh rather than the sword that has power to destroy the flesh, that fear you fear will come upon you, and what you dread will happen.

There is nothing hidden that is not to be revealed, nothing

secret that will not be known [Luke 12:2; Matt. 10:26]. When the works of darkness are brought to light, they will be accused by the light, and not only abominable hidden obscenities, but also the wicked business of men who sell mysteries for money and the fraudulent whisperings of men who invent deceits and pervert judgment. All these will he who knows everything, who sees into the heart and bowels, reveal, when he begins to bring lamps to Jerusalem.

What therefore will they do, or rather what will they suffer, those who have committed sins, when they hear, "Go into everlasting fire," you who have not done good works? When will he be admitted to the wedding feast, he who has neither girded his loins to abstain from evil nor kept his light burning to do good? Then neither the integrity of virginity nor the brightness of the lamp will be able to excuse the lack of one thing: the oil [Matt. 25:1]. Or what tortures must be believed to lie in wait for those who in this life have done not merely wrong, but perhaps the worst of evils, if those who have received good things here are to be so tormented that in the midst of the flames their burning tongues are not cooled by even one tiny drop of water [Luke 16:24]?

Let us therefore beware of wrongdoing, and let us not commit sins freely within the Church, trusting that it casts a wide net, knowing that fishermen do not keep everything the net brings in, but when the boat comes to shore they choose the good fish and throw away the bad. Let us not be content to gird our loins. Let us also light our lamps and be conscientious in doing good works, bearing it in mind that every tree, not only the one that bears bad fruit but also the one that does not bear good fruit, will be cut

down and thrown into the fire, that "eternal fire that has been prepared for the devil and his angels" [Matt. 25:41].

For the rest, let us so turn our backs on evil and do good that we
may seek peace and not glory. For glory is God's, and he will not
yield it to anyone else. "My glory," he says, "I will not give to
another" [Isa. 42:8; 48:11]. And it was a man after God's heart
who said, "Not unto us, O Lord, not unto us, but to thy name give
glory" [Ps. 115:1]. Let us remember too what Scripture says, "If
you offer aright and do not divide rightly, you have sinned" [Gen.
4:7]. This "division" of ours is right, brothers; let no man question
it. If there is anyone who is displeased by it, let him know that it is
not we who make it but the angels. It was the angels who first
sang, "Glory to God in the highest and peace on earth to men of
goodwill" [Luke 2:14].

Let us therefore keep oil in our vessels, lest (perish the thought)
we beat in vain on the doors of the wedding feast when they are
already closed and hear the dread word of the Bridegroom answering us from within, "I do not know you" [Matt. 25:12]. Death
stands beside the entrance still, not only of unrighteousness,
unfruitfulness, and vanity, but also of pleasure itself. That is why we
need fortitude against the temptation to sin, so that, strong in the
faith, we may resist the roaring lion and with this shield manfully
repel his fiery arrows. We need justice to do good. We need pru-
dence, so that we may not be reproved with the foolish virgins.
Last, we need temperance, so that we do not, in the midst of our
pleasures, one day hear what that wretched man heard, when,
feasts and fine garments set aside, he prayed for mercy and heard,
"Remember, son, that you have received good things in your life

and Lazarus bad things; now he is comforted and you are tormented" [Luke 16:25]. How terrible is God in his counsels concerning the sons of men! But if he is terrible, he is also merciful when he does not hide the nature of the judgment that is to come. "The soul that has sinned will die" [Ezek. 18:4]. The branch that has not borne fruit will be cut off [John 15:2]. The virgin who has no oil shall be shut out of the wedding feast [Matt. 25:12]; and he who has received good things in this life will be tormented in the life to come [Luke 16:25]. If perhaps all these four are to be found in anyone, his state is clearly very desperate.

That the flesh resists the spirit that is beginning to fear God and trying to do good

The reason suggests these things inwardly to the will the more abundantly as it is taught the more fully by the illumination of the Spirit. Happy indeed is he whose will has given itself up and taken the advice of reason, so that, although at first it is fearful, afterwards it is cherished by heavenly promises and brings forth the spirit of salvation.

But perchance the will is found rebellious and obstinate and not merely impatient, but, worse, after warnings, impervious to threats and prickly when flattered. Perhaps it will be found that the will is not moved at all by the suggestions of reason and replies with a flash of anger, "How long am I to endure you? Your preaching does not move me. I know that you are clever, but your cleverness does not fool me." Perhaps, then, the will, calling upon the members of the body one by one, urges them harder than ever to give in to their desires and act wickedly. That is an only too familiar daily experience to all of us, that those who are giving their minds to conversion are tempted the more strongly by the desires of the flesh, and those who seek to leave Egypt and escape from Pharaoh are driven harder to make bricks out of clay [Exod. 1:14; 5:19–21].

Would that such a one might turn aside from ungodliness and be careful not to fall into that terrible abyss of which it is written, "The ungodly man thinks nothing of it when he comes to the depths of wickedness" [Prov. 18:3]. He can be cured only by the most powerful remedy, and he will easily fail, unless he takes care to follow the physician's advice and do what he tells him. The temptation is fierce. It brings a man close to desperation, unless he gathers all his forces to take pity on his soul, which he sees to be so wretched and pitiable, changes his attitude, and listens to the voice of him who says, "Blessed are they who mourn, for they shall be comforted" [Matt. 5:4].

Let him mourn abundantly, for the time for mourning has come and his state is greatly to be wept over. Let him mourn, but not without holy love and in hope of consolation. Let him bear in mind that he can find no rest in himself, but all is full of misery and desolation. Let him bear it in mind that there is no good in his own flesh, and that this wicked world offers nothing but vanity and affliction of spirit. Let him consider, I say, that neither within nor beneath nor around him is any consolation to be found, so that at last he may learn to seek what is to be sought above and to hope for what comes from above. Yet let him mourn meanwhile, bewailing his sorrow. Let his eyes pour out water. Let his eyelids not close in sleep. Truly, the eye that was in darkness before is cleansed by tears and its sight sharpened, so that it is able to gaze into the brightness of that most serene light.

After grief comes comfort and the kindling of the desire to contemplate heavenly things

From now onward, let him gaze upward through the window, look out through the lattice, and follow the guiding star with all his attention; and, zealously imitating the Magi, let him seek the Light in the light [Ps. 36:9]. He will find a wonderful place to pitch his tent [Ps. 42:4], where a man may eat the bread of angels [Ps. 78:25]. He will find a paradise of pleasure planted by the Lord. He will find a garden of sweet flowers. He will find a cool resting place, and he will say, "O that that wretched will would listen to my voice, so that it might enter in and see these good things and visit that place! Here indeed will it find further rest, and it will disturb me less when it is itself less disturbed." For he speaks the truth who says, "Take my yoke upon you and you will find rest for your souls" [Matt. 11:29].

Trusting in this promise, she addresses the angry will more soothingly and with a cheerful expression, and in the spirit of gentleness which befits her says, "Do not be indignant. I am not able to cause you to stumble. I am your body; your own self. There is nothing to fear or to dread."

Do not be surprised if the will's reply is more bitter than ever. It says, "Too much thinking has made you mad" [Acts 26:24]. For the moment, let the reason wait quietly and hide its doings, until, talking of this and that, it can bring the subject up opportunely, saying, "Today I discovered a most beautiful garden, a very pleasant place. It would be good for us to be there. For it does you harm to be tossed on this bed of sickness, to be turning over your sorrow on your bed, to be grieving heavy-hearted in your chamber. The Lord will be near to him who seeks him, to the soul who hopes in him. He will attend to the vows of his suppliants, and he will minister to them in the power of his word." The will's desire will be moved, and not only to see the place; it will also long to enter it, little by little, and make its dwelling there.

How resting in this contemplation the soul delights in the taste of Him and learns from Him

Do not think that this inward paradise of pleasure is corporeal. It is not with the feet but with the affections that a man enters it. Nor is it the plentifulness of earthly trees that makes it desirable to you, but the joyous and lovely plantation of spiritual virtues that grows there. It is an enclosed garden, where a sealed fountain gives forth four springs [Song of Sgs. 4:12] and a fourfold virtue comes from a single source of wisdom. There too the whitest lilies spring, and when the flowers appear the voice of the turtledove is heard. There the perfume of the Bride gives off a most sweet fragrance, and other scents abound. There the north wind is still, and the south wind softly blows [Song of Sgs. 1:12; 4:16]. There in the midst is the Tree of Life, the apple tree of the Song of Songs, more precious than all the trees of the wood, in whose shade the Bride finds coolness and whose fruit is sweet to her taste.

There continence shines, and the vision of pure truth illuminates the eye of the heart. The most sweet voice of the inner Comforter brings joy and gladness to the ears. There the most lovely odor of a fruitful field that the Lord has blessed is carried to the nostrils of hope. There a foretaste of the incomparable delights of love is enjoyed, and the mind, anointed with mercy and freed from the sharp thorns and briars by which it was once pricked, rests happily with a clear conscience.

These are not among the rewards of eternal life. They should be thought of as wages of the soldiering of this life. They do not belong to what is promised to the Church in the future, but rather to what she is promised now. For this is the hundredfold reward that is set before those who despise the world.

You do not need any speech of mine to commend this to you; the Spirit reveals it himself. You do not need to look it up in the pages of a book. Look to experience instead. Man does not know the price of wisdom. It comes from hidden places, and it has a sweetness with which no sweetness known to living men can compare. It is the sweetness of the Lord, and you will not recognize it unless you taste it. "Taste and see," he says, "how sweet the Lord is" [Ps. 34:8].

The new name that a man knows only if he receives it is hidden manna [Rev. 2:17]. Not learning but anointing teaches it; it is not grasped by knowledge but by conscience. It is holy. It is a pearl. He who began both to do and to teach will not himself do what he forbids. For he does not think of those who have renounced their former sins and wickednesses as dogs or swine. They are even comforted by the Apostle, who says, "Some of you were like this, but you have been washed and you are sanctified" [1 Cor. 6:11]. But let the dog be careful not to return to his vomit and the sow not to go back to wallowing in the mire.

Having tasted such food, the soul understands that they are blessed who hunger and thirst after righteousness

Therefore in this gate of paradise the voice of the divine whisper is heard, a most holy and secret counsel, which is hidden from the wise and prudent and revealed to little children. When it hears this voice, reason not only grasps what it says but communicates it readily to the will. "Blessed are they who hunger and thirst after righteousness, for they shall be filled" [Matt. 5:6]. It is the supreme advice, and a mystery beyond thinking of. It is "a faithful saying and worthy to be received by everyone" [1 Tim. 1:15; 4:9] that he who came to us from heaven came from a royal throne. For there was a great famine on earth, and we did not only all come to be in need; we are brought to an extremity of need. That is, we are compared with brute beasts and become like them. We even hunger insatiably for the husks the pigs eat.

He who loves money is not satisfied; he who loves luxury is not satisfied; he who loves glory is not satisfied; in short, he who loves the world is never satisfied. I myself have known men sated with this world and sickened by every memory of it. I have known men sated with money, sated with honors, sated with the pleasures and curiosities of this world, and more than a little: to the point of nausea. And by the grace of God it is easy for every one of us to be sated in this way! For it is a satiety produced not by abundance but by contempt. So, foolish sons of Adam, devouring the husks intended for the pigs, you are feeding not your hungry souls but the hunger itself. Indeed, we continue to lack food when we sit at this banquet; unnatural food only sustains hunger. And, to take a plainer example, that of one of the many things human vanity desires, I tell you that man's heart is not satisfied with gold any more than his body is satisfied with wind. Let the miser not be indignant. The same thing is true of the ambitious, the luxurious, and the criminal. If perhaps there is anyone who does not believe me, let him believe experience: his own or that of many others.

Which of you, brothers, desires to be satisfied and to have his desire fulfilled? Let him begin to hunger after righteousness, and he cannot fail to be satisfied. Let him desire that bread of which there is plenty in his Father's house, and he will find that the husks of the pigs disgust him. Let him try to taste righteousness even a little, for the more he desires it, the more will he deserve it; it is written, "He who eats me will hunger for more, and he who drinks me will thirst for more" [Sir. 24:21]. For this desire is more in keeping with the spirit of man. It takes possession of the human heart with a more natural and more powerful desire and energetically casts out all other desires. So the strong-armed man is driven out by a stronger, as a nail can often be driven out by a nail. "Blessed therefore are those who hunger and thirst after righteousness, for they shall be satisfied" [Matt. 5:6]. Not yet indeed with that which a man shall be filled with and live, but with all the other things that had been desired insatiably before, so that from now on the will shall cease to sell the body into slavery and its former lusts, and expose it to the influence of reason. Instead, it will urge it to continue in righteousness, so as to grow with no less zeal than it showed before when it served infirmity unto iniquity.

That our sins, once punished, are forgiven and, if they are not repeated, cannot be a stumbling block, but rather work together for good

And now the will has been changed and the body brought into subjection to it, as though the fountain of evil had been dried up in part and the opening covered over. The third task remains, and that is the hardest: to purify the memory and pump out the cesspit. How can I forget my own life? Take a thin piece of poor-quality parchment that has soaked up the ink with which the scribe has written on it. Can any skill erase it? It is not merely superficially colored; the ink is ingrained. It would be pointless for me to try to clean it. The parchment would tear before the marks of wretchedness were removed. Forgetting would perhaps destroy the memory itself, so that, in a mental convulsion, I should cease to remember what I had done.

We must ask, then, what keen edge can both clean my memory and keep it intact? Only the living and effective Word, which is sharper than a two-edged sword, which "takes away your sins" [Mark 2:5]. The Pharisee may murmur and say, "Who can take away sins except God?" [Mark 2:7; Luke 5:21]. He who says this to me is God, and no one else is to be compared with him. He set out the whole way of discipline; he gave it to his servant Jacob and to his beloved Israel; and after that he was seen on earth and talked with men. His pardon wipes out sin, not from the memory, but in such a way that what before was both present in the memory and rendered it unclean is now, although it is still in the memory, no longer a defilement to it. For now many sins come to mind that we know to have been committed by ourselves or by others. But it is our own sins that defile the memory; those of others do not hurt it. Why is this, if not because it is our own sins that cause us shame? These are what we fear to have charged against us. Take away condemnation, take away fear, take away confusion, and there is full remission of sins. Then our sins will not be against us, but will work together for good, so that we may give devout thanks to him who has remitted them.

On the mercy promised to the penitent and wretched; "Blessed," he says, "are the merciful"

For him who prays for mercy, there is a fitting reply. "Blessed are the merciful, for they shall obtain mercy" [Matt. 5:7]. Have mercy on your own soul if you want God to have mercy on you. Drench your bed in tears night after night, and remember to water your couch with weeping. If you take compassion on yourself, if you labor with groans of repentance—for this is your first step in mercy—you will indeed find mercy. If you are perhaps a great sinner with many sins, and you ask a great mercy and many acts of pity, you too must strive to show great mercy. Be reconciled to yourself, for you did yourself grave injury in setting yourself up against God.

Now that peace has been restored in your own house, it is necessary first to extend it to your neighbor, that he may give you a new kiss with the kiss of his mouth [Song of Sgs. 1:2]; as it is written, you must be reconciled and at peace with God. Forgive those who have sinned against you, and your own sins will be forgiven you; and you will pray to the Father with a quiet conscience, and say, "Forgive us our sins as we forgive those who sin against us" [Matt. 6:12].

If perhaps you have cheated anyone, make good what you owe and give what is left over to the poor, and you will be shown mercy. "If your sins were as scarlet, they shall be as white as snow, and if they were red as vermilion, they shall be white as wool" [Isa. 1:18]. So that you may not be put to shame for all the devices of your wrongdoing, for which you blush now, give alms, and if you cannot do so from your earthly substance, do it from your goodwill, and they will all be clean. Not only will the reason be enlightened and the will put right, but the memory itself will be purged, and henceforth you will cry to the Lord and hear a voice saying, "Blessed are the pure in heart, for they shall see God" [Matt. 5:8].

That the heart must be cleansed if the soul is to see God, for "Blessed are the pure in heart"

"Blessed are the pure in heart, for they shall see God" [Matt. 5:8]. This is a great promise, my brothers, and something to be desired

with all one's heart. For to see in this way is to be like God, as John
the Apostle says: "Now we are all sons of God, but it has not yet
been made clear what we shall be. For we know that when it is
made clear we shall be like him, for we shall see him as he is" [1
John 3:2]. This vision is eternal life, as Truth himself says in the
Gospel, "This is eternal life, that they should know that you alone
are the true God, and him whom you have sent, Jesus Christ"
[John 17:3].

Hateful is the blemish that deprives us of this blessed vision.
Detestable is the neglectfulness that causes us to put off the cleans-
ing of the eye. For just as our bodily vision is impeded either by a
humor within or by dust from outside entering the eye, so too is
our spiritual vision disturbed by the desires of our own flesh or by
worldly curiosity and ambition. Our own experience teaches us
this, no less than the Sacred Page, where it is written, "The body
that is corruptible weighs down the soul, and the earthly habitation
oppresses its thoughts" [Wisd. of Sol. 9:15]. But in both it is sin
alone that dulls and confuses the vision; nothing else seems to stand
between the eye and the light, between God and man. For while we
are in this body, we are in exile from the Lord.

That is not the body's fault, except in that it is yet mortal; rather,
it is the flesh that is a sinful body, the flesh in which is no good
thing but rather the law of sin reigns. Meanwhile the bodily eye
[Gen. 27:1], when the mote is no longer in it [Matt. 7:4] but has
been taken or blown away, still seems dark, as he who walks in the
spirit and sees deeply often experiences. For you will cure a
wounded limb quickly by withdrawing the sword, but only if you
apply poultices to heal it. For no one should think himself cleansed

because he has come out of the cesspit. No, rather let him realize that he stands in need of a thorough washing first. Nor must he be washed only with water; he needs to be purged and refined by fire so as to say, "We have passed through fire and water, and you have brought us to a resting place" [Ps. 66:12]. "Blessed are the pure in heart, for they shall see God" [Matt. 5:8]. "Now we see through a glass darkly, but hereafter face-to-face" [1 Cor. 13:12]. Then truly our faces will be completely clean, so that he may present them to himself shining, without stain or wrinkle.

Of the peacemaker at peace and making peace; "Blessed are the peacemakers"

Here there follows immediately and appropriately, "Blessed are the peacemakers, for they shall be called the children of God" [Matt. 5:9]. A man is in a state of peace when he renders good for good, as far as it lies in him to do, and wishes harm to no one. There is another kind of man who is patient; he does not render evil for evil, and he is able to bear injury. Then there is the peacemaker, who returns good for evil and is ready to do good even to someone who harms him. The first is a little child and easily tripped up. In this evil world he will not readily be saved. The second, as it is written, possesses his own soul in patience. The third not only possesses his own soul, but also wins the souls of many others. The first possesses peace, as far as it lies in him to do so. The second holds fast to peace. The third makes peace. He, then, is deservedly blessed with the name "son," because he does the work of a son, for, grateful for his own reconciliation, he reconciles others to his Father too. So he who has served well gains for himself a good position; there can be no better place in the Father's house than that of his son. "For if sons, then heirs, heirs of God and co-heirs with Christ" [Rom. 8:17], so that, as he himself says, where he is, there may his servant be too.

We have wearied you by talking for so long, and we have kept you longer than we should have done. Now time puts an end to our loquacity, as shame has not.

But remember what the Apostle said; we read that he once went on preaching until midnight [Acts 20:7]. "Would to God," to use his words, "that you could bear with a little of my folly. For I care jealously for your good as God himself does" [2 Cor. 11:1–2].

An attack upon the ambitious who presume to bring God's peace to others before their own hearts are pure

Little children, "who made it clear to you that you should flee from the wrath to come?" [Matt. 3:7; Luke 3:7]. For no one deserves anger more than the enemy who pretends friendship: "Judas, do you betray the Son of Man with a kiss?" [Luke 22:48]. You, a man of one mind with him, who used to take pleasant meals with him, whose hand dipped into the same dish, you have no part in the prayer with which he prays to the Father and says, "Father, forgive them, for they do not know what they are doing" [Luke 23:34]. Woe to you who take away the key not only of knowledge but also of authority; you do not enter in yourself and in many ways you prevent those you ought to introduce from entering in. You steal the keys rather than receiving them. The Lord asks about such through the prophet: "They have reigned, but not by me. They have chosen princes, but I did not call them to the thrones they occupy" [Hos. 8:4].

Whence comes such zeal for preferment, such shameless ambition, such folly of human presumption? Surely none of us would dare to take over the ministry of any earthly king, even the most minor, without his instructions (especially when he actually prohibits it) or to seize his benefices or conduct his affairs? Do not suppose, then, that God will approve of what he endures from those in his great house who are vessels fit for destruction.

Many come, but consider who is called. Listen to the Lord's words in their order. "Blessed," he says, "are the pure in heart, for they shall see God," and then, "Blessed are the peacemakers, for they shall be called the children of God" [Matt. 5:9]. The heavenly Father calls the pure in heart, who do not seek for themselves, but for Christ, and not what will profit them, but what will profit many. "Peter," he says, "do you love me?" "Lord, you know that I love you." "Feed my sheep," he replies [Matt. 5:48ff.]. For when would he commit such beloved sheep to someone who did not love them? This question of who is found to be a faithful servant is much debated among clerks.

Woe to unfaithful stewards who, themselves not yet reconciled, take on themselves the responsibility for recognizing righteousness in others, as if they were themselves righteous men. Woe to the sons of wrath who profess that they are ministers of grace. Woe to the sons of wrath who are not afraid to usurp to themselves the rank and name of "peacemaker." Woe to the sons of wrath who pretend to be mediators of peace and who feed on the sins of the people. Woe to those who, walking in the flesh, cannot please God and presume to wish to please him.

The startling usurpation of the highest rank of peacemaker by those who have not reached the lower ranks, not even the first

We do not wonder, my brothers, we who take pity on the present state of the Church; we do not wonder at the basilisk that arises from the serpent root [Isa. 14:29]. We do not wonder if he who wanders from the way the Lord has laid down steals the grapes from the Lord's vineyard. For the man who has not yet heard in his heart the voice of the Lord calling him, or if perhaps he begins to hear it, he takes flight back into the undergrowth to hide, impudently appropriates the rank of peacemaker and takes the place that belongs to a son of God. As a result he has not yet stopped sinning, but is still dragging a long rope. He has not yet become a man who perceives his own poverty. He says, "I am rich, and in need of nothing," although he is poor, naked, wretched, and pitiable. He has nothing of the spirit of gentleness with which he could instruct those who are caught in sin, bearing in mind his own susceptibility to temptation.

He knows nothing of tears of compunction. Rather, he rejoices when he has done wrong and exults in his worst deeds. He is one of those to whom the Lord says, "Woe to you who laugh now, for you will weep" [Luke 6:25]. He desires money, not justice. His eyes are caught by anything showy. He hungers insatiably for honor and thirsts for human glory. He has no bowels of mercy [Col. 3:12]. Rather, he rejoices in his anger and behaves like a tyrant. He seeks to make a profit from piety. What am I to say about the purity of his heart? Would that he had not given it over to forgetfulness like a dead man who has no thoughts. Would that he were not a "dove gone astray and having no heart" [Hos. 7:11]. The bodily garment is found to be stained; would that even the outside were clean, so that he could obey at least in part him who says, "Be clean, you who bear the vessels of God" [Isa. 52:11].

That the incontinent do not fear boldly to take holy order

Although we do not accuse everyone, yet we cannot excuse everyone. The Lord has left himself many thousands. Otherwise, if their righteousness did not excuse us and the Lord of Sabaoth had not left us a holy seed, we should have been overwhelmed long ago like Sodom and punished like Gomorrah [Jer. 50:40].

The Church seems to have grown. Even the most holy order of the clergy is multiplied beyond counting. But even if you have multiplied the people, Lord, you have not made joy greater, and merit seems to have decreased as much as numbers have increased. Everywhere people are rushing to join sacred orders, and they seize with neither reverence nor consideration upon ministries the angels themselves regard with veneration. For the ungodly do not fear to take up the banner of the heavenly kingdom or to wear the crown of its jurisdiction, men in whom greed rules, ambition gives the orders, pride holds sway, iniquity is enthroned, lust is the principal ruler. If, following the prophecy of Ezekiel, we were to dig under the wall to see something horrible in God's house, in these men the worst abomination would perhaps appear within the walls. Truly, having committed fornication, adultery, and incest, some do not fail to go on to ignominious passions and nameless deeds. Would that these things (which are still the same breach of proper behavior) were not still being committed today. Would that the Apostle did not need to write these things, nor we to speak of them. Would that when we speak of such abominable things ever crossing any man's mind, no one would believe us.

Is it not true that those cities that gave rise to this filth were once foredoomed by divine judgment and destroyed by fire [Gen. 19:24ff.]? Did not the flame of hell, unable to wait, come to destroy that accursed nation because its sins were an outstanding eyesore and went before it to judgment? Did not that fire and sulfur and that stormy wind wipe out the land as if aware of such confusion? Was it not all reduced to nothing more than a dreadful lake? The five heads of the hydra were cut off, but alas, countless more sprang up. Who has rebuilt the cities of vice? Who has widened their walls of shame? Who has spread their poisonous offspring over the earth? Woe, woe, the enemy of men has strewn the wretched remnants of that sulfurous burning all around; with its disgusting ashes he has sprinkled the body of the Church, and even some of her ministers too with its most fetid and foul matter!

Alas, "a chosen people, a royal priesthood, a holy nation, a people for possession" [1 Pet. 2:9], who at first were flowing with the divine and spiritual graces of the Christian religion, is it to be believed that such things could ever be found in you?

Marked with this stain they enter the tabernacle of the living God [Deut. 5:26]. With this mark on them they dwell in his temple, polluting the Lord's holy place; they will receive a multiple condemnation, because they carry such burdened consciences and nevertheless enter God's sanctuary. Such not only do not please God; they anger him when they seem to be saying in their hearts, "He will require it" [Ps. 10:13]. They anger him a good deal and set him against themselves, and I fear that they do so in the very acts that ought to bring them closer to him.

Would that, when they were about to begin to build the tower, they would sit down and count the cost in case they do not have enough to finish it. Would that those who cannot contain themselves stood in fear of rashly professing a state of perfection or taking the name of celibates. It is a costly tower indeed, and a great word, which not all can accept. But it would undoubtedly be better to marry than to burn, and to remain in the lower rank of the faithful people and be saved than to live a worse life in the high rank of the clergy and be judged the more severely. For many—not all, but still many, so many that they certainly cannot be hidden, nor in their impudence do they want to be—many seem to have bestowed the freedom in which they were called upon the flesh, abstaining from the remedy of marriage and then wallowing in wickedness.

Exhortation to repentance and to seek a humble place first, and only after becoming worthy to look to higher honor

Spare your souls, I beg you, brothers, spare them; spare the blood shed for you. Beware of the fearful danger; turn from the fire that is prepared. Do not let the profession of perfection turn out to be a mockery. Let virtue take a straightforward form in holiness. Do not let the form of the celibate life be vain and empty of truth. Does chastity not stand in danger from pleasure, humility from riches, piety from worldly business, truth from chattering, love from this wicked world? Flee from the midst of Babylon, flee and save your souls. Fly to the cities of refuge, where you can do penance for past sins and also obtain grace in the present and confidently await future glory. Let not consciousness of sins hold you back, for where sins abound, grace abounds the more. Let not the severity of penance deter you, for the sufferings of this present time are nothing in comparison with past sin, which is forgiven, or with the glory to come that is promised to us. And there is no bitterness that the prophet's meal cannot sweeten or wisdom, the Tree of Life, make delicious.

If you do not believe words, believe deeds. Accept the evidence of many men's example. Sinners rush from all sides to repent, and those delicate by habit and nature alike think nothing of outward discomfort if it eases the gnawing of their conscience. Nothing is impossible to those who believe. Nothing is difficult for those who love. Nothing is harsh to the meek. Nothing is hard to the humble, who are assisted by grace and whose obedience is under the tender command of devotion.

Why do you walk in great and wonderful things that are beyond you? It is a great and wonderful thing to be a minister of Christ and a steward of God's mysteries. The order of peacemakers is far above you, unless perhaps you prefer to leap, rather than climb, and leave out the stages that come first. Would that he who enters in that way could administer as faithfully as he confidently pushed his way in. But it is difficult, perhaps impossible, for the sweet fruit of love to ripen from the bitter root of ambition. I say to you, yet not I but the Lord, "When you are called to the wedding feast sit down in the lowest place, for everyone who exalts himself will be humbled and he who humbles himself will be exalted" [Luke 14:8–10].

On the endurance of persecution according to the last beatitude, "Blessed are those who suffer persecution"

"Blessed," he says, "are the peacemakers, for they shall be called the children of God." Consider carefully that it is not the people who call for peace, but those who make peace who are commended. For there are those who talk but do nothing. For just as it is not the hearers of the law but the doers who are righteous, so it is not those who preach peace but the authors of peace who are blessed. Would that today's Pharisees—for perhaps there are some—would at least say what they ought, even if they do not do it. Would that those who do not wish to preach the Gospel unless they are paid might at least preach it for money. Would that they preached the Gospel if only so that they could eat!

"The hireling," the Bible says, "sees the wolf coming and flees" [John 10:12]. Oh, that those who are not shepherds today would show themselves to be hirelings in charge of the sheep and not wolves. Would that they did not themselves injure the sheep and flee when no one is pursuing. Would that they might not expose the flock to danger when they see the wolf coming. They had to be endured when they were found, especially in time of peace, receiving their pay and, if only for the money, working to guard the sheep: as long as they themselves did not disturb the sheep and drive them away from the pastures of righteousness and truth for nothing. But persecution separates and distinguishes the hirelings from the shepherds beyond question. For when did he who seeks worldly reward not fear passing losses? When did he who wants money more than righteousness endure worldly persecution for righteousness' sake? "The blessed," he says, "are those who suffer persecution for righteousness' sake, for theirs is the kingdom of heaven" [Matt. 5:10]. This happiness belongs to shepherds, not hirelings. Far less is it the reward of robbers or wolves. They do not suffer persecution for righteousness' sake so much as preferring to endure persecution rather than maintain righteousness. Truly, it is contrary to their way of working; it troubles them even to hear of it.

For the rest, you can see men ready to stir up trouble, to bear hatred, to pretend to be ashamed, to ignore curses, to undergo all risks for the sake of avarice and ambition; no less ruinous is the animosity of men like that than the feebleness of hirelings. Their own good shepherd who was ready to lay down his life for the sheep says to the shepherds, "Blessed shall you be when men shall hate you and when they shall separate you and cast out your name as evil, for the Son of Man's sake. Be glad and rejoice when that happens, for your reward is great in heaven" [Luke 6:22].

Those whose treasure is in heaven have no reason to fear. There is no reason for them to complain about many tribulations when they are confident of a manifold reward. No, let them rather rejoice, as is fitting, that it is not so much persecution that is increased as reward, and let them rejoice the more that they bear many things for Christ, so that with him henceforth a more abundant reward may wait for them. "Why are you fearful, O ye of little faith?" [Matt. 8:26]. The faithful word stands firm on the changeless truth, for no adversity can hurt you if no wickedness has you in its control. But it is a small thing that it will not hurt you; it will even profit you, and abundantly, as long as righteousness is your purpose and Christ is your cause, with whom "the patience of the poor will never perish" [Ps. 9:18]. To him be glory now and forever, world without end.

ON LOVING GOD

Aimeric, cardinal deacon of the Church of Rome from 1121 and chancellor from 1126, was a good friend to Clairvaux. Bernard wrote him more than a dozen letters. Sometime between 1125 and 1141 Aimeric asked him for a book on loving God. Early in the 1120s Bernard had already written on the love of God in the context of the monastic life in a letter to the Carthusian monks of the Grande Chartreuse, written at their request. His thinking in "On Loving God" is close to what he said there, although developed in more detail. He had evidently been pleased with the way he had expressed the central ideas in this letter, for he instructed that it be copied at the end of the new treatise. The whole treatise, including the letter, is translated here, as Bernard himself would have wished. The letter is integral to what he has to say.

—G. R. EVANS

Prologue

To the illustrious lord Aimeric, cardinal deacon and chancellor of the See of Rome, Bernard, called abbot of Clairvaux, wishes that he may live for the Lord and die in the Lord.

You usually ask me for prayers, not answers to questions. And indeed I confess that I am not worthy to offer either. Yet prayer is my profession, even if I do not live as though it were. As to the task you have given me, to tell the truth it seems to me that I lack the diligence and ability it requires. Still, I assure you that I am glad you are asking for spiritual in return for wordly gifts. It is only that you could have asked someone richer in spiritual gifts than I.

Because it is the habit both of the educated and of the uneducated to make this sort of excuse, you would be hard put to it to know whether it is prompted by genuine inability or self-excusing modesty, were it not that the execution of the task will make it plain. Accept from my poverty what I have, or I shall be thought a philosopher because of my silence.

I do not promise to answer everything you ask—only to tell you what God will give me to say about loving him. This subject tastes sweeter, is treated with more confidence, and is more profitable to whoever hears than any other. Your other questions you must keep for those better qualified to answer them.

You wish, then, to hear from me why and how God ought to be loved. I answer: The cause of loving God is God himself. The way to love him is without measure. Is this not enough? Perhaps it is, but only for the wise. Yet I owe something to the unwise too, and it is usual to add something for their benefit to what is sufficient for the wise man. And so, for the sake of those who are slower, I shall not find it tedious to go into each point at length, if not more deeply.

For two reasons, then, I say that God is to be loved for his own sake. No one can be more justly loved or with greater benefit. Indeed, when it is asked why God ought to be loved, the question has two possible meanings. We may wonder which is the real question: whether God is to be loved because he deserves it, or because it is for our good. I give the same answer to both: There seems to me no good reason to love him that does not lie in himself. So let us first see how he deserves our love.

How God is to be loved for his own sake

He who gave himself to us when we did not deserve it certainly deserves a great deal from us. What better thing could he give us than himself? And so if we bring God's deserving into question in asking why God should be loved, we have the chief reason for loving him in this, "That he first loved us" [1 John 4:9–10]. Surely he deserves to be loved in return when we think of who loves, whom he loves, how much he loves. Is it not he to whom every spirit confesses, saying, "You are my God, for you do not need the goods I have" [Ps. 16:2]?

This divine love is true love, for it is the love of one who wants nothing for himself. To whom is such pure love shown? "When we were still his enemies," it says, "he reconciled us to himself" [Rom. 5:10]. So, in utmost generosity, God loved even his enemies.

But how much did he love? St. John says, "God so loved the

world that he gave his only begotten Son" [John 3:16]. St. Paul says, "He did not spare his own Son, but gave him up for us" [Rom. 8:32]. The Son too said of himself, "No one has greater love than the man who lays down his life for his friends" [John 15:13]. Thus the righteous deserved to be loved by the wicked, the highest and all-powerful by the weak.

But someone says, "That is true for men, but not for angels." It is true; he who came to man's help in his great need preserved the angels from that need; he who did not allow men to remain as they were out of an equal love gave the angels the grace not to fall into such a need.

To those who see these things clearly, I think it will be evident why God is to be loved—and why he deserves to be loved. But if unbelievers hide these facts, God is always able to make their ingratitude plain by the innumerable kindnesses he showers on men for their benefit, which are quite obviously his gifts. For who else provides food for everyone who eats, light for seeing, air to breathe? It would be foolish to want to list them when I have just said that they are innumerable. Let it be enough to give the chief ones, bread, sun, and air, as examples. I say "chief" not because they are more excellent than other gifts, but because they are more necessary, for they are bodily necessities.

You must look for higher goods in the higher part of yourself, that is, the soul. These higher goods are dignity, knowledge, virtue. Man's dignity is his free will, which is the gift by which he is superior to the animals and even rules them. Man's knowledge is that by which he recognizes that he possesses this dignity, but that it does not originate in himself. His virtue is that by which he seeks eagerly for his Creator and, when he finds him, holds to him with all his might.

Each of these three has two aspects. Dignity is not only a natural privilege. It is also the power of dominion, for all living things on earth can be seen to stand in fear of man. Knowledge too is twofold, for we know both that we possess this dignity and whatever else we have that is good, and that they do not originate in ourselves. Virtue can equally be seen to have two aspects. By it we seek our Maker, and when we have found him we cling to him so that we cannot be separated from him.

Dignity is nothing without knowledge, and knowledge can even be a stumbling block without virtue. This is the reason for both these things. What glory is it to have what you do not know you have? And to know what you have, but not to know that it does not originate with you is to have glory, but not before God. To him who glories in himself the Apostle says, "What do you have that you have not received? But if you have received it, why do you boast as if you had not received it?" [1 Cor. 4:7]. He does not simply say, "Why do you boast?" He adds, "As if you had not received," so as to emphasize that the guilt lies not in boasting of something, but in doing so as if it was not a gift that had been received. This sort of thing is rightly called vainglory, because it does not rest on a solid foundation of truth. St. Paul points out the difference between truth and vainglory: "He who boasts, let him boast in the Lord" [1 Cor. 1:31; 2 Cor. 10:17; cf. Jer. 9:23–24], that is, in the truth. For the Lord himself is truth.

There are two things you should know: first, what you are; second, that you are not what you are by your own power. Then you will boast, but not in vain. It says that if you do not know yourself, you should go and follow the flocks of your companions. This is what actually happens. When man has a high honor bestowed on him but does not appreciate it, he is deservedly compared with the beasts, with whom he shares his present mortality and state of corruption.

It happens too when a man does not appreciate the gift of reason and spends his time with herds of unreasoning beasts; and when he ignores the glory that is within him and models himself on the outward things his senses perceive; and when he is so carried away by curiosity that he becomes no different from any other animal, because he does not see that he has received anything more than they have.

And so we should greatly fear the ignorance that makes us think less of ourselves than we should. But no less, indeed rather more, should we fear the ignorance that makes us think ourselves better than we are. This is what happens when we are deceived into thinking that some good in us originates with ourselves.

But you should avoid and detest even more than these two that presumption by which, in full knowledge and deliberately, you dare to seek your own glory in good things that are not your own and that you know perfectly well are not yours by any power of your own. Thus you unashamedly steal another's glory. For the first ignorance has no glory. The second has a glory, but not in God's eyes. But this third evil that is committed knowingly is an act of treason against God.

This arrogance born of the last ignorance is worse and more dangerous because, although the second kind of ignorance causes us to ignore God, this leads us to despise him. And it is worse and more disgusting than the first because, although the first makes us the companions of beasts, this throws us into fellowship with demons. It is pride, the greatest sin, to use gifts you have been given as though you were born with them, and to arrogate to yourself the glory that belongs to the generous Giver.

With these two, dignity and knowledge, must go virtue, which is the fruit of both. Through virtue we seek and cling to the Giver of all good things and give him the glory he deserves for all that he has given. But he who knows how to do what is right and does not do it will receive many lashes [Luke 12:47]. Why? Because "he did not want to understand how to behave well" [Ps. 36:3]. More than that, "He plotted wickedness upon his bed" [Ps. 36:4]. He endeavors like a wicked servant to snatch and steal away the good Lord's glory for himself, the glory due for the good qualities he knows quite certainly do not originate with himself, because God has given him that knowledge.

It is perfectly obvious then that without knowledge dignity is utterly useless, and that knowledge without virtue is to be condemned. Truly the man of virtue, in whom knowledge is not to be condemned and dignity is not fruitless, cries to God and freely confesses, "Not to us, Lord, but to your name be the glory" [Ps. 115:1]. That is, "We credit ourselves with no knowledge or dignity; we ascribe it all to your name, for it all comes from you."

We have wandered too far from our subject in striving to show that those who do not know Christ are without excuse, for they are taught enough by natural law and the good perceptions of their bodily senses to oblige them to love God for his own sake. To sum up what has been said: Is there anyone, even an unbeliever, who does not know that he has received the necessities of bodily life in this world, which we mentioned earlier—by means of which he survives, sees, and breathes—from no other but him who gives food to all flesh, who causes his sun to rise on the good and the wicked alike, and the rain to fall on the just and the unjust? Again, what man, however wicked, would think that the human dignity that shines in his soul came from any Author but he who says in Genesis, "Let us make man in our own image and likeness" [Gen. 1:26]? Who can think that the Giver of knowledge is anyone but he who teaches man knowledge? And who either thinks he has received the gift of virtue from any but the hand of that same Lord of virtues or hopes to have it from any other source?

And so God deserves to be loved for himself, even by the unbeliever, for even if he does not know Christ, he knows himself. No one, not even an unbeliever, can be excused, if he does not love God with all his heart, all his mind, and all his strength. An inborn sense of justice in him, which reason recognizes, cries out that he ought to love him with all his powers, for he knows that he owes him everything.

Yet it is difficult for anyone, once he has received from God the power to will freely, to give up his will wholly to God and not rather to will things for himself. Perhaps it is impossible. He is tempted to treat what he has been given as his own and clutch it to himself, as it is written, "Everyone seeks his own" [Phil. 2:21], and again, "The thoughts and feelings of men are inclined to evil" [Gen. 8:21].

On the contrary, the faithful know how utterly they stand in need of Jesus and him crucified. They wonder at and reach out to that supreme love of his, which passes all knowledge. They are ashamed not to respond to such love and deserving with the little they have to give.

The more surely you know yourself loved, the easier you will find it to love in return. Those to whom less has been given love less. The Jew and the pagan are not moved by such wounds of love as the Church experiences. She says, "I am wounded by love" [Song of Sgs. 5:8], and again, "Surround me with flowers, pile up apples around me, for I am sick with love" [Song of Sgs. 2:5]. The Church sees King Solomon in the crown his mother had placed on his head. She sees the Father's only Son carrying his cross. She sees the Lord of majesty struck and spat upon. She sees the Author of life and glory transfixed by nails, wounded by a lance, smeared with abuse, and finally laying down his precious life for his friends. She sees these things, and the sword of love pierces her soul more deeply, and she says, "Surround me with flowers, pile up apples around me, for I am sick with love" [Song of Sgs. 2:5].

Where do the pomegranates come from?

These are beyond a doubt the pomegranate fruits that the Bride brought into her Beloved's garden [Song of Sgs. 6:11]. They were picked from the Tree of Life, and their taste had been transmuted to that of the heavenly bread, and their color to that of Christ's blood. At last she sees the death of death and death's author defeated. She sees captivity led captive from hell to earth and from earth to heaven, so that at the name of Jesus every knee may bow, in heaven, on earth, and in hell. Under the ancient curse the earth had produced thorns and thistles; now she sees it burst into bloom again under the renewed grace of a new blessing. And as she beholds all this, she remembers the verse "My flesh has bloomed again, and willingly shall I praise him" [Ps. 28:7]. She desires to add to the pomegranate fruits that she gathered from the tree of the cross some of the flowers of the resurrection, whose fragrance more than anything else invites the Bridegroom to visit her more often.

Next she says, "You are fair, my Beloved, and beautiful. Our bed is strewn with flowers" [Song of Sgs. 1:16]. By the mention of the bed she makes it plain enough what she desires; and when she says that it is strewn with flowers, she indicates clearly why she hopes to be granted her desire: not for her own merits, but for the sake of flowers from the field the Lord has blessed. Christ delighted in flowers. He wanted to be conceived and to grow up in Nazareth. The heavenly Bridegroom takes such pleasure in these fragrances that he comes often and willingly to the chamber of the heart in which he finds such fruits piled up and such flowers strewn. Where, that is, he sees constant reflection on the grace of the Passion and the glory of the resurrection. There he is present constantly and willingly.

The tokens of the Passion are like last year's fruits, the fruits, that is, of all the time past that was spent under the dominion of sin and death. In the fullness of time they appear. But see, the signs of the resurrection are like the flowers of a new age, blooming in a new summer of grace; and their fruit will be the general resurrection, which is to come at the last and which will last forever. "Now," it says, "winter is over. The rain is past and gone. Flowers appear in our land" [Song of Sgs. 2:11–12]. This means that summer has come, with him who changed the coldness of death into the warm spring of a new life. "Behold," he says, "I will make all things new" [Rev. 21:5]. His flesh was sown in death; it flowered again in the resurrection. His fragrance makes the dry grass grow green again in the fields of our "valley." What was cold becomes warm again. What was dead comes to life again.

In the freshness of these flowers and fruits and the beauty of the field, which gives off so sweet a scent, the Father himself takes delight in the Son, who is making all things new, so that he says, "Behold the odor of my Son is like that of a rich field that the Lord has blessed" [Gen. 27:27], a rich field indeed, of whose fullness we have all received.

The Bride enjoys a greater freedom, for she may gather fruit and pick the flowers when she wishes. With these she strews her conscience within, so that when the Bridegroom comes, the couch of her heart may give off a sweet fragrance.

It befits us too to fortify our own hearts with the testimony of faith, if we want Christ to be a frequent guest: faith both in the mercy of him who died for us and in the power of him who rose again, as David said, "I have heard these two things: Power is of God, and mercy is yours, Lord" [Ps. 62:11–12]. And so the "testimonies" of both these things "are utterly believable" [Ps. 93:5]. Christ died for our sins and rose again to make us righteous. For our protection he ascended and sent the Holy Spirit to be our Comforter. He will one day return to bring us fulfillment. He showed his mercy in dying, his power in the resurrection, and both in the remainder of his actions.

With these fruits and flowers the Bride begs to be surrounded and nourished now. I believe that she does so sensing that the warmth of her love can easily cool if it is not encouraged and supported until she is led into the chamber [Song of Sgs. 2:4; 3:4], where she will be held in the long-desired embrace, so that she can say, "His left hand is under my head and his right hand has embraced me" [Song of Sgs. 2:6].

Then she will know and experience indeed all the testimonies of love she has received at his first coming, as though from the left hand of the Beloved and far less sweet and of less worth than the embrace of his right hand. She will experience what she has heard, "The flesh is of no value; it is the spirit that gives life" [John 6:64]. She will prove in reality what she has heard, "My spirit is sweeter than honey, and my inheritance than honey and the honeycomb" [Sir. 24:20], and what follows: "The memory of me will endure forever" [Sir. 39:9]. This means that as long as this world lasts, in which one generation is succeeded by another, God's chosen ones will not be without the consolation of memory until they can enjoy the feast of God's presence. Thus it is written, "They will broadcast the memory of your sweetness" [Ps. 145:7], referring undoubtedly to those of whom it is said just before this passage, "Generation after generation will praise your works" [Ps. 145:4]. And so memory is for the generations of this world; presence belongs to the kingdom of heaven. Those who are chosen already enjoy the glory of his presence there; the generation that is still on its pilgrimage is comforted in the meantime by memory.

It is important to note which generation takes comfort in remembering God. It is not the wicked and stubborn generation, to whom it is said, "Woe to you who are rich; you have your consolation" [Luke 6:24], but rather the generation that can say, "My soul refused to be comforted" [Ps. 77:2]. This is truly our attitude if we add what follows: "I remembered the Lord and rejoiced" [Ps. 77:3]. It is indeed right that those who take no delight in present things should be sustained by the recollection of what is to come, and those who refuse to be consoled by plentiful but mutable things should find joy in thinking of eternity. This is the generation of those who seek the Lord, who do not look for their own advantage, but seek the face of the God of Jacob.

In the meantime memory is sweet for those who long for God's presence. It does not satisfy their longing, but intensifies it. He himself bears witness to the manner of his feeding: "He who eats me will hunger for more" [Sir. 24:21]. And he who is fed by God says, "I shall be satisfied at the sight of your glory" [Ps. 17:15].

Blessed are those who are hungry and thirsty for righteousness now, for they alone will be satisfied one day. Woe to you, wicked and perverse generation! Woe to you, stupid and foolish people, who do not trouble to think of the past, and who fear the future! Not even now do you want to be freed from the snare of the hunters, for those who wish to become rich in this world fall into the devil's net. Even then you cannot avoid the harsh words. Oh, the harsh and cruel sentence, "Go, you who are cursed, into everlasting fire!" [Matt. 25:41]. These words are harsher and more dreadful than what is repeated every day for us in Church in the memorial of his Passion, "He who eats my flesh and drinks my blood has eternal life" [John 6:55]. That is, "He who remembers my death and mortifies his members on earth after my example has eternal life" [John 3:36]. That means, "If we suffer together, you shall reign with me" [Rom. 8:17; 2 Tim. 2:12].

And yet many today shrink back at these words and desert him, and answer not in words but by their actions, "This is a hard saying. Who can listen to it?" [John 6:61]. The generation that did not discipline its heart and whose spirit is not in good credit with God, but that hopes instead in unreliable riches, feels oppressed by the story of the cross and thinks it burdensome to remember the Passion. How will it ever bear the weight of his words when it actually hears them, "Go, you who are cursed, into everlasting fire, which is prepared for the devil and his angels" [Matt. 25:41]? This stone will crush him on whom it falls.

But truly the generation of the righteous will be blessed, those who, whether away from him or in his presence, strive with the Apostle to please God. They will hear, "Come, you blessed of my Father," and so forth. Then the generation that did not discipline its heart will learn too late how easy and sweet in comparison with that sorrow was Christ's burden, from which they withdrew their stiff necks as if it were a rough, hard load.

O wretched slaves of mammon, you cannot simultaneously glory in the cross of our Lord Jesus Christ and hope for a treasury of money or chase after gold, and taste how sweet the Lord is. So then, you will doubtless find him whom you did not find sweet to remember severe indeed when you stand before him in person.

By contrast the faithful soul sighs deeply for his presence and rests peacefully in the thought of him, and until it is fit to have the glory of God revealed to it face-to-face, it glories in the ignominy of the cross. So then does the Bride and Dove of Christ wait. In the meantime she rests upon her inheritance; for there fall to her lot now in the present, in the recollection of the abundance of your sweetness, Lord Jesus, silvery wings, candid with innocence and purity. She places her hope in the joy she will feel at the sight of your face. Then even her back will gleam gold, when she is led with delight into the splendor of the saints. There the rays of wisdom will illuminate her more brightly still.

Rightly indeed does she glory now and say, "His left hand is beneath my head, and his right hand embraces me" [Song of Sgs. 2:6]. His left hand stands for the recollection of his love, than which nothing is greater, for he laid down his life for his friends. His right hand signifies the blessed vision he promised to his friends and the joys of the presence of his majesty. Rightly too that vision of God that makes us resemble him, that inestimable delight in the divine presence, is thought of as the "right hand," of which the Psalmist sings in delight, "In your right hand are everlasting joys" [Ps. 16:11]. In the "left hand" we rightly "place" that wonderful love that is recollected and is always to be remembered, for the Bride leans upon it and rests until evil is past.

Rightly then is the left hand of the Bridegroom under the Bride's head, upon which he supports her leaning head. This leaning is the intention of her mind, and he supports it so that it may not bend or incline toward fleshly and worldly desires. For the body, which is corruptible, weighs down the soul, and the earthly dwelling of the soul hems it in and keeps it preoccupied with many thoughts.

What is the result of contemplating such great mercy and mercy so undeserved, such generous and proven love, such unlooked-for condescension, such persistent gentleness, such astonishing sweetness? To what, I ask, will all these wonderfully draw and deeply attract the thoughtful mind when it considers them carefully and is wholly set at liberty from unworthy love? It will despise everything else, everything that will get in the way of that desire. The Bride surely runs eagerly in the odor of these perfumes and loves ardently. Yet even when she has fallen wholly in love, she thinks she loves too little because she is loved so much. And she is right. What can repay so great a love and such a lover? It is as if a little speck of dust were to marshal itself to return a love that is ever before it in majesty and that can be seen to bend all its power on the work of salvation. The words "God so loved the world that he gave his only begotten Son" [John 3:16] were certainly spoken of the Father, and "He gave himself up to death" [Isa. 53:12] was undoubtedly said of the Son [John 14:26]. And it is said of the Holy Spirit, "The Paraclete, the Holy Spirit, whom my Father will send in my name, he will teach you all things and will cause you to remember all that I have said to you" [John 14:26]. God, then, loves, and loves with all his being, for the whole Trinity loves—if the word "whole" can be used of the infinite, the incomprehensible, absolute Being.

I believe that he who understands this will recognize clearly enough why God is to be loved, that is, why he deserves to be loved. Because the Son is not his, the unbeliever has neither the Father nor the Holy Spirit. For, "He who does not honor the Son does not honor the Father who sent him" [John 5:53]. Nor does he honor the Holy Spirit whom the Son sent. And so it is not surprising that a man

should love the less someone whom he knows less well. Nevertheless, the unbeliever is aware that he owes him everything, because he
knows that he is the Author of everything.

But then what of me? What do I owe, who hold my God to be
not only the generous Giver of my life, its beneficent Governor, its
holy Comforter, its careful Director, and above all these, its most
liberal Redeemer, everlasting Protector, Defender, Glorifier? It is
written, "With him is plentiful redemption" [Ps. 130:7], and
again, "He entered the sanctuary once and for all, when he had
won eternal salvation" [Heb. 9:12]. And, on conversion, "He will
not forsake his own; they shall be kept safe forever" [Ps. 37:28].
And the Gospel says about the riches he brings, "They will pour
into your lap good measure, full and pressed down and running
over" [Luke 6:38]. And again, "Eye has not seen or ear heard, nor
has it entered the mind of man, what God has prepared for those
who love him" [1 Cor. 2:9]. And about glorification, "We wait for
the Savior, our Lord Jesus Christ, who will renew the body of our
lowliness and make it like his glorified body" [Phil. 3:20–21].
And, "The sufferings of this time are not to be compared with the
glory that is to come, which will be revealed in us" [Rom. 8:18],
and again, "That which is but a brief and light trouble in this present life will work in us beyond its weight, for eternal life, as we
contemplate not the things that are seen but the things that are
unseen" [2 Cor. 4:17–18].

What shall I give to God in return for all these things? Reason
and natural justice press the unbeliever to give himself up wholly
to him from whom he has everything and to love him with all his
heart. Faith urges me to love more than that him whom I know to

have given me not only myself but his own self. When the age of faith had not yet come, God had not made himself known in the flesh, died on the cross, risen from the tomb, returned to the Father, or proved his great love for us, about which I have said so much; when he had not yet commanded man to love the Lord his God with all his heart, with all his soul, and with all his strength, that is, with all he is, all he knows, all he can do.

God is not unjust when he claims his works and his gifts for himself. Why should the work of an artist not love its master, if it has the ability to do so? Why should it not love him with all its might, since it can do nothing except by his gift?

In addition, the fact that man was created gratuitously, out of nothing—and in such dignity—makes the duty of love still clearer and demonstrates further the justice of God's demand. Besides, think of the greatness of the additional kindness when he saved man and beast. How did God multiply his mercy then? We, I emphasize, exchanged our glory for the likeness of a calf, which eats grass, and have become like brute beasts through our sins. If I owe all that I am in return for my creation, what am I to add in return for being remade, and remade in this way? For I was not remade as easily as I was made. It is written not only of me, but of everything that was made, "He spoke and they were made" [Ps. 148:5]. But he who made me by speaking once said a great deal more to remake me, and did miracles and endured hardship, and not only hardship but humiliation. "What then shall I give the Lord for all that he has given me?" [Ps. 116:12]. In the first act he gave me myself; in the second he gave himself; and when he did that he gave me back myself. Given and given again, I owe myself in return for myself, twice over. What am I to give God in return for himself? For even if I could give myself a thousand times over, what am I to God?

How God should be loved

First, see in what measure God deserves to be loved by us, and how he deserves to be loved without measure. For (to repeat briefly what I have said), "He first loved us" [1 John 4:10]. He loved—with such love, and so much and so generously—us who are so insignificant and who are what we are. I remember I said at the beginning that the way to love God was to love without measure. Now since the love that is directed to God is directed to something immense, something infinite (for God is both immense and infinite)—who, I ask, ought to draw a line to our love or measure it out? And what about the fact that our love itself is not freely given, but given in payment for a debt? So immensity loves; eternity loves; the love that passes knowledge gives itself; God loves, whose greatness knows no bounds, whose wisdom cannot be counted, whose peace passes all understanding. And do we measure out our response?

"I will love you, Lord, my strength, my fortress, my refuge, my deliverer" [Ps. 18:1–2], you who are everything I can desire and love. My God, my Helper, I shall love you in proportion to your gift and my capacity, less indeed than is just, but to do that is beyond me. Even though I cannot love you as much as I ought, still I cannot love you more than I am able. I shall be able to love you more only when you deign to give me more; and even then you can never find my love worthy. "Your eyes have seen my imperfection," and "all shall be written down in your book" [Ps. 139:16], all who do what they can, even if they cannot do all that they should. It is clear, I think, how much God ought to be loved, and for what merit in him. For his own merit, I say. But to whom is it really clear how great that is? Who can say? Who can feel it?

Now let us see how he is to be loved for our benefit. How far does our perception of him fall short of what he is? We must not keep silent about what we can see clearly, even if all is not clear to us. Above, when we proposed to seek why and how God is to be loved, I said that there were two meanings of the question with which we began. We asked why he should be loved, meaning by what merit of his or for what benefit of ours. Both questions can, it seems, be asked. After speaking of God's merit, not as he deserves, but as well as I am able, it remains for me to say something about the reward, as far as it will be given to me to do.

That God is not loved without reward

God is not loved without reward, even though he should be loved without thought of reward. True charity cannot be empty, but it does not seek profit, "for it does not seek its own benefit" [1 Cor. 13:5]. It is an affection, not a contract. It is not given or received by agreement. It is given freely; it makes us spontaneous. True love is content. It has its reward in what it loves. For if you seem to love something, but really love it for the sake of something else, you actually love what you are pursuing as your real end, not what is a means to it. Paul did not preach in order to eat; he ate in order to preach. He loved not the food, but the Gospel.

True love does not ask for a reward, but it deserves it. A reward is offered to him who does not yet love; it is owed to him who loves; it is given to him who perseveres. When we are trying to persuade people about lesser matters, it is not the willing but the unwilling whom we woo with promises and rewards. Who would think a man ought to be paid for doing what he wants to do? No one, for example, pays a hungry man to eat, or a thirsty man to drink, or a mother to feed the child of her womb. Who would think of getting someone to fence his vine or dig round his tree or build himself a house by begging him to do it or paying him a fee? How much more does the soul that loves God ask for no reward but God? Certainly, if that is not all it asks, it does not love God.

It is always natural for every rational being to desire what it sees to be finer and to direct its energies toward it. It is never satisfied with anything that lacks what it judges it should have. For example, a man who has a beautiful wife looks at a lovelier woman with a discontented eye or mind. He who is dressed in fine clothes wants better. He who is very rich envies a richer man.

Today you see many men who already have great wealth and possessions still laboring day by day to add one field to another and to extend their boundaries—with greed that knows no bounds. And you see those who have houses worthy of a king and vast palaces nevertheless adding house to house every day and building with a restless love of novelty, knocking down what they build, altering rectangles to rounds. And what of men in high positions? Do we not see them striving with all their might to reach still higher positions? Their ambition is never satisfied. There is no end to it all because the highest and the best is not to be found in any of these things. If a man cannot be at peace until he has the highest and best, is it surprising that he is not content with inferior and worse things? It is folly and extreme madness always to be longing for things that not only can never satisfy but cannot even blunt the appetite; however much you have of such things, you still desire what you have not yet attained; you are always restlessly sighing after what is missing.

When the wandering mind is always rushing about in empty effort among the various and deceptive delights of the world, it grows weary and remains dissatisfied. It is like a starving man who thinks that whatever he is stuffing himself with is nothing in comparison with what remains to be eaten; he is always anxiously wanting what he does not have rather than enjoying what he has. For who can have everything? The little that a man obtains by all his effort he possesses in fear. He does not know what he will lose and when.

Thus the perverted will that is aiming for the best and trying to make speed toward what will fully satisfy it fails in its endeavor. Vanity makes fun of it, bringing it into these twisted paths; sin deceives itself with lies. If you really wish to have what you desire, that is, if you wish to lay hold of what leaves nothing further to be desired, what need is there to bother with these other things? If you do, you are running along winding roads, and you will be dead long before you reach what you desire by this route.

The wicked therefore walk around in this circle, naturally wanting what will satisfy their wants and foolishly thrusting away the means of attaining it—that is, of attaining not consumption but consummation. In this way they wear themselves out with point-less effort and do not reach the end of happy fulfillment. They delight in the beauty of the creature rather than of the Creator. They lust for each and every experience more than they desire to come to the Lord of all. And indeed if they could ever do all they set themselves to do, they would succeed—if anyone could indeed obtain everything without the Source of all things.

For by the law of human desire that causes man to hunger more for the things he does not have than for the things he has, and to spurn what he has for the sake of things he does not possess, soon he has obtained and cast aside everything in heaven and on earth. In the end, I do not doubt that he will rush toward the only thing he now lacks—the God of all. There he will rest, for just as there is no rest this side of heaven, so on the other side nothing can disturb his rest.

Then he will surely say, "It is good for me to cling to God" [Ps. 73:28]. He will say, "What is there for me in heaven, and what have I desired on earth?" [Ps. 73:25]. And again, "God of my heart, God, my lot forever" [Ps. 73:26]. So therefore, as I said, whoever desires the greatest good can reach it, if he can first gain all the other things he wants that fall short of it.

But that is quite impossible. Life is too short. Our strength is insufficient. There are too many temptations. Those who struggle on are exhausted by the length of the roads and the uselessness of their efforts. They wish to obtain all they want, but they are unable to reach the end of their desires. If they would only be content with reaching it all in thought and not insist on experiencing it!

That they can easily do, and it would not be pointless, for man's mind is quicker than his senses and it sees farther, and the senses dare not touch anything the mind has not already examined and approved. I think this is what is meant by the text "Test everything, and hold on to what is good" [1 Thess. 5:21]. The mind looks ahead, and if it does not give permission, the senses must not pursue what they want. If they did, you would not go up the mountain of the Lord, nor stand in his holy place, and you would have received your rational soul in vain; you would be following your sense like a dumb beast without any resistance from your lazy reason. Those whose reason does not keep ahead of their feet run, but not on the road. They spurn the Apostle's advice. They do not run to win. When will they reach him whom they put off coming to until they have tried everything else? The desire to possess everything first is a winding road and a circle to go around and around forever.

The just man is not like that. When he hears about the wicked behavior of those who are going round and round—for there are many traveling the wide road that leads to death—he chooses for himself the royal road and turns neither right nor left. Finally, the prophet bears witness, "The path of the just is straight and straight-forward to walk on" [Isa. 26:7]. It is men such as this who take the shortcut to salvation and avoid the troublesome and unrewarding roundabout way, choosing the brief and abbreviating word. They do not want to have everything they see. On the contrary, they sell all they have and give it to the poor. "Blessed are the poor," indeed, "for theirs is the kingdom of heaven" [Matt. 5:3]. Everyone runs, but we must distinguish between the runners. For "The Lord knows the way of the just; the way of the wicked will perish" [Ps. 1:6]. So a little is better to the just than all their wealth is to the wicked, for indeed—as Wisdom says and the foolish man discovers—"He who loves money will not be satisfied by money" [cf. Eccl. 5:9]. But those who hunger and thirst after righteousness will be satisfied.

Righteousness is the natural and vital food of the rational soul. Money cannot diminish the mind's hunger; more than air is needed to satisfy that of the body. If a hungry man opens his mouth to the wind and you see him blow out his cheeks with air in the hope of satisfying his hunger, will you not think he is mad? So it is no less a madness if you think the rational soul can be satisfied and not merely "puffed up" by bodily things. What do bodily things mean to the soul? The body cannot feed on spiritual things or the soul on bodily things. "Bless the Lord, my soul. He satisfies your desire with good things" [Ps. 103:1, 5]. He satisfies it with good things, stirs it to goodness, keeps it in goodness, anticipates, sustains, fulfills. He causes you to desire, and he himself satisfies your desire.

I said before that God is the cause of loving God. I spoke the truth, for he is both the efficient and the final cause. He himself provides the occasion. He himself creates the longing. He himself fulfills the desire. He himself causes himself to be (or, rather, to be made) such that he should be loved. He hopes to be so happily loved that no one will love him in vain. His love both prepares and rewards ours. Kindly, he leads the way. He repays us justly. He is our sweet hope. He is riches to all who call upon him. There is nothing better than himself. He gave himself in merit. He keeps himself to be our reward. He gives himself as food for holy souls. He sold himself to redeem the captives.

Lord, you are good to the soul that seeks you. What are you then to the soul that finds? But this is the most wonderful thing, that no one can seek you who has not already found you. You therefore seek to be found so that you may be sought for, sought so that you may be found. You can be sought and found, but not forestalled. For even if we say, "In the morning my prayer will forestall you" [Ps. 88:13], it is certain that every prayer that is not inspired is half-hearted.

Now let us see where our love begins, for we have seen where it finds its end.

Love is one of the four natural passions. They are well enough known; there is no need to name them. It is clearly right that what is natural should be at the service of the Lord of nature. That is why the first and great commandment is, "You shall love the Lord your God" [Matt. 22:37].

The first degree of love: When man loves himself for his own sake

But because nature has become rather frail and weak, man is driven by necessity to serve nature first. This results in bodily love, by which man loves himself for his own sake. He does not yet know anything but himself, as it is written, "First came what is animal, then what is spiritual" [1 Cor. 15:46]. This love is not imposed by rule, but is innate in nature. For who hates his own flesh? But if that same love begins to get out of proportion and headstrong, as often happens, and it ceases to be satisfied to run in the narrow channel of its needs, but floods out on all sides into the fields of pleasure, then the overflow can be stopped at once by the commandment "You shall love your neighbor as yourself" [Matt. 22:39].

It is wholly right that he who is your fellow in nature should not be cut off from you in grace, especially in the grace that is innate in nature. If a man feels it a heavy burden to help his brothers in their need and to share in their pleasures, let him keep his desires in check all by himself if he does not want to fall into sin. He can indulge himself as much as he likes as long as he remembers to show an equal tolerance to his neighbor. O man, the laws of life and discipline impose restraint to prevent you chasing after your desires until you perish, and to save you from making of nature's good things a way to serve the soul's enemy through lust.

Is it not much more right and honest to share nature's goods with your fellow man, that is, your neighbor, than with an enemy? If you take the advice of Wisdom and turn away from your pleasures and make yourself content with food and clothing as the Apostle teaches, soon you will find that your love is not impeded by carnal desires that fight against the soul. I think you will not find it a burden to share with your fellow man what you withhold from the enemy of your soul. Then will your love be sober and just, when you do not deny your brother what he needs from the pleasures you have denied yourself. It is in this way that bodily love is shared, when it is extended to the community.

But what are you to do, if when you share with your neighbor, you yourself are left without something you need? What but ask in full faith from him who gives generously to everyone and does not grudge, who opens his hand and pours blessing on every creature. There is no doubt that he will come to your aid generously when you are in need, since he is so generous in time of plenty. Scripture says, "First seek the kingdom of God and his justice, and all these things will be added to you" [Matt. 6:33; Luke 12:31]. He promises without being asked to give what is needed to whoever is not greedy for himself and loves his neighbor. This is to seek the kingdom of God and to implore his help against the tyranny of sin, to take on the yoke of chastity and sobriety rather than to let sin rule in your mortal body. More: This is righteousness, to share what is common to your nature with him who has the same gift of nature.

But to love one's neighbor with perfect justice it is necessary to be prompted by God. How can you love your neighbor with purity if you do not love him in God? But he who does not love God cannot love in God. You must first love God, so that in him you can love your neighbor too.

God therefore brings about your love for him, just as he causes other goods. This is how he does it: He who made nature also protects it. For it was so created that it needs its Creator as its Protector, so that what could not have come into existence without him cannot continue in existence without him. So that no rational creature might be in ignorance of this fact and (dreadful thought) claim for himself the gifts of the Creator, that same Creator willed by a high and saving counsel that man should endure tribulation; then when man fails and God comes to his aid and sets him free, man will honor God as he deserves. For this is what he says: "Call upon me in the day of tribulation. I will deliver you, and you shall honor me" [Ps. 50:15]. And so in that way it comes about that man, who is a bodily animal and does not know how to love anything but himself, begins to love God for his own benefit, because he learns from frequent experience that in God he can do everything that is good for him and that without him he can do nothing.

The second degree of love: When man loves God for his own good

Man therefore loves God, but as yet he loves him for his own sake, not God's. Nevertheless the wise man ought to know what he can do by himself and what he can do only with God's help; then you will avoid hurting him who keeps you from harm.

If a man has a great many tribulations and as a result he frequently turns to God and frequently experiences God's liberation, surely even if he had a breast of iron or a heart of stone, must he not soften toward the generosity of the Redeemer and love God not only for his own benefit, but for himself?

The third degree of love: When man loves God for God's sake

Man's frequent needs make it necessary for him to call upon God often, to taste by frequent contact, and to discover by tasting how sweet the Lord is. It is in this way that the taste of his own sweetness leads us to love God in purity more than our need alone would prompt us to do. The Samaritans set us an example when they said to the woman who told them the Lord was there, "Now we believe, not because of your words, but because we have heard him for ourselves and we know that truly he is the Savior of the world" [John 4:42]. In the same way, I urge, let us follow their example and rightly say to our flesh, "Now we love God not because he meets your needs; but we have tasted and we know how sweet the Lord is" [Ps. 34:8].

There is a need of the flesh that speaks out, and the body tells by its actions of the kindnesses it has experienced. And so it will not be difficult for the man who has had that experience to keep the commandment to love his neighbor. He truly loves God, and therefore he loves what is God's. He loves chastely, and to the chaste it is no burden to keep the commandments; the heart grows purer in the obedience of love, as it is written. Such a man loves justly and willingly keeps the just law.

This love is acceptable because it is given freely. It is chaste because it is not made up of words or talk, but of truth and action. It is just because it gives back what it has received. For he who loves in this way loves as he is loved. He loves, seeking in return not what is his own, but what is Jesus Christ's, just as he has sought not his own but our good or, rather, our very selves. He who says "we trust in the Lord, for he is good" [Ps. 118:1] loves in this way. He who trusts in the Lord not because he is good to him but simply because he is good truly loves God for God's sake and not for his own. He of whom it is said "he will praise you when you do him favors" [Ps. 49:18] does not love in this way.

That is the third degree of love, in which God is already loved for his own sake.

The fourth degree of love: When man loves himself for the sake of God

Happy is he who has been found worthy to attain to the fourth degree, where man loves himself only for God's sake. "O God, your justice is like the mountains of God" [Ps. 36:6]. That love is a mountain, and a high mountain of God. Truly, "a rich and fertile mountain" [Ps. 68:15]. "Who will climb the mountain of the Lord?" [Ps. 24:3]. "Who will give me wings like a dove, and I shall fly there and rest?" [Ps. 55:6]. That place was made a place of peace, and it has its dwelling place in Zion. "Alas for me, my exile has been prolonged!" [Ps. 120:6]. When will flesh and blood, this vessel of clay, this earthly dwelling, grasp this? When will it experience this kind of love, so that the mind, drunk with divine love and forgetting itself, making itself like a broken vessel, throw itself wholly on God and, clinging to God, become one with him in spirit and say, "My body and my heart have fainted, O God of my heart; God, my part in eternity" [Ps. 73:26]? I should call him blessed and holy to whom it is given to experience even for a single instant something that is rare indeed in this life. To lose yourself as though you did not exist and to have no sense of yourself, to be emptied out of yourself and almost annihilated, belongs to heavenly, not human, love.

And if indeed any mortal is rapt for a moment or is, so to speak, admitted for a moment to this union, at once the world presses itself on him, the day's wickedness troubles him, the mortal body weighs him down, bodily needs distract him, he fails because of the weakness of his corruption, and—more powerfully than these—brotherly love calls him back. Alas, he is forced to come back to himself, to fall again into his affairs, and to cry out wretchedly, "Lord, I endure violence; fight back for me" [Isa. 38:14], and, "Unhappy man that I am, who will free me from the body of this death?" [Rom. 7:24].

But since Scripture says that God made everything for himself, there will be a time when he will cause everything to conform to its Maker and be in harmony with him. In the meantime, we must make this our desire: that as God himself willed that everything should be for himself, so we too will that nothing, not even ourselves, may be or have been except for him, that is, according to his will, not ours. The satisfaction of our needs will not bring us happiness, not chance delights, as does the sight of his will being fulfilled in us and in everything that concerns us. This is what we ask every day in prayer when we say, "Your will be done, on earth as it is in heaven" [Matt. 6:10]. O holy and chaste love! O sweet and tender affection! O pure and sinless intention of the will—the more pure and sinless in that there is no mixture of self-will in it, the more sweet and tender in that everything it feels is divine.

To love in this way is to become like God. As a drop of water seems to disappear completely in a quantity of wine, taking the wine's flavor and color; as red-hot iron becomes indistinguishable from the glow of fire and its own original form disappears; as air suffused with the light of the sun seems transformed into the brightness of the light, as if it were itself light rather than merely lit up; so, in those who are holy, it is necessary for human affection to dissolve in some ineffable way and be poured into the will of God. How will God be all in all if anything of man remains in man? The substance remains, but in another form, with another glory, another power.

When will this be? Who will see this? Who will possess it? "When shall I come and when shall I appear in God's presence?" [Ps. 42:2]. O Lord my God, "My heart said to you, 'My face has sought you. Lord, I will seek your face'" [Ps. 27:8]. Shall I see your holy temple?

I think that cannot be until I do as I am bid. "Love the Lord your God with all your heart and with all your soul and with all your strength" [Mark 12:30]. Then the mind will not have to think of the body. The soul will no longer have to give the body life and feeling, and its power will be set free of these ties and strengthened by the power of God. For it is impossible to draw together all that is in you and turn toward the face of God as long as the care of the weak and miserable body demands one's attention. So it is in a spiritual and immortal body, a perfect body, beautiful and at peace and subject to the spirit in all things, that the soul hopes to attain the fourth degree of love, or rather to be caught up to it; for it lies in God's power to give to whom he will. It is not to be obtained by human effort. That, I say, is when a man will easily reach the fourth degree: when no entanglements of the flesh hold him back and no troubles will disturb him, as he hurries with great speed and eagerness to the joy of the Lord.

But do we not think that the holy martyrs received this grace while they were still in their victorious bodies—at least in part?

They were so moved within by the great force of their love that they were able to expose their bodies to outward torments and think nothing of them. The sensation of outward pain could do no more than whisper across the surface of their tranquillity; it could not disturb it.

But what of those who are already free of the body? We believe that they are wholly immersed in that sea of eternal light and bright eternity.

What is impossible for souls before the resurrection

It is not in dispute that they want their bodies back; if they thus desire and hope for them, it is clear that they have not wholly turned from themselves, for it is evident that they are still clinging to something that is their own, even if their desires return to it only a very little. Until death is swallowed up in victory and the everlasting light invades the farthest bounds of night and shines everywhere—so that heavenly glory gleams even in bodies—these souls cannot wholly remove themselves and transport themselves to God. They are still too much bound to their bodies, if not in life and feeling, certainly in natural affection. They do not wish to be complete without them, and indeed they cannot.

And so, before the restoration of their bodies, souls will not lose themselves, as they will when they are perfect and reach their highest state. If they did so, the soul would be complete without its body and would cease to want it. The body is not laid down nor resumed except for the good of the soul. "Precious in God's sight is the death of his saints" [Ps. 116:15].

If death is precious, what must life be, and life such as that? It need not be surprising that the glorified body should seem to confer something on the soul, for it was of use to it when it was weak and mortal. Oh, how truly did he speak who said that all things work together for good to those who love God! Its weak body helps the soul to love God; it helps it when it is dead; it helps it when it is resurrected, first in producing fruits of patience, second in bringing peace, third in bringing completeness. Truly the soul does not want to be perfected without what it feels has served it well in every condition.

It is clear that the flesh is a good and faithful companion to the good spirit. It helps it if it is burdened, or if it does not help, it relieves it; at any rate, it is an aid and not a burden. The first state is full of labor, but fruitful; the second is a time of waiting, but without weariness; the third is glorious. Listen to the Bridegroom in the Song holding out this threefold invitation: "Eat," he says, "and drink, friends; be intoxicated, dearest" [Song of Sgs. 5:1]. He calls those who are laboring in the body to eat. Those who have set aside their bodies he calls to drink. Those who have resumed their bodies, he encourages to drink their fill. These he calls "dearest," for they are filled to overflowing with love. For there is this difference between these and those others he calls "friends," not "dearest," so that those who groan because they are still laboring in the flesh are held dear for the love they have; those who are free from the weight of the flesh are more dear because they are made more ready and quicker to love. More than both are they called "dearest" (and so they are) who, having received the second garment, are in their resurrected bodies in glory. They burn the more eagerly and fiercely with love for God, because nothing is now left to them that can trouble them or hold them back in any way. Neither of the first two states can claim that. For in the first the body is born along with labor, and in the second too it is awaited with no small desire.

First, then, the faithful soul eats its bread but, alas, in the sweat of its brow. While in the flesh the soul moves by faith, which must act through love, for if it does not, it is dead.

This work is food; as the Lord says, "My food is to do the will of my Father" [John 4:34]. When it is free of the flesh, the soul no longer feeds on the bread of sorrow but, having eaten it, is allowed to drink deeply of the wine of love, but not the pure wine, for as it says in the Song of Songs in the person of the Bride, "I drank my wine mixed with milk" [Song of Sgs. 5:1]. The soul mixes the sweetness of natural affection with the wine of divine love when it desires to resume its glorified body. The soul therefore burns when it has drunk the wine of holy charity, but not to the point of intoxication, for the admixture of this milk tempers it for the moment. Intoxication overthrows minds and makes them forget everything. The soul that is still concerned with the restoration of its body is not forgetting itself completely. But after it finds the only thing it needs, what is to prevent it from taking leave of itself altogether, going to God, and becoming as much unlike itself as it is given to it to be like God? Then only is the soul allowed to drink from the goblet of wisdom, of which we read, "How splendid is my cup that intoxicates me" [Ps. 23:5]. Is it surprising if the soul is then intoxicated by the riches of God's dwelling? No longer tormented by wordly cares, it safely drinks the pure new wine with Christ in his Father's house.

Wisdom presides over this threefold banquet of love, feeding those who labor, giving drink to those at rest, and intoxicating those who rule. As at a banquet in this world, food is served before drink, as the order of nature requires, and Wisdom keeps to it.

First, up to the time of our death, we eat the work of our hands, when we chew effortfully what has to be swallowed. After death, in the spiritual life, we drink with ease whatever we are offered. Then, when our bodies are resurrected, we are intoxicated by immortal life, abounding in wonderful plenty. This is what the Bridegroom means in the Song, "Eat and drink, friends; be intoxicated, dearest" [Song of Sgs. 5:1].

Dearest indeed, who are intoxicated with love. Intoxicated indeed, who deserve to be present at the wedding feast of the Lord, eating and drinking at his table in his kingdom, when he takes his Church to him in glory, without blemish or wrinkle or any defect. Then will he intoxicate his dearest ones with the torrent of his delight, for in the most passionate and most chaste embrace of Bridegroom and Bride, the rush of the river makes glad the city of God. I think this is none other than what the Son of God, who waits on us as he goes, promised: "The just are feasting and rejoicing in the sight of God, and they delight in their gladness" [Ps. 68:3]. Here is fullness without disgust, insatiable curiosity that is not restless, an eternal and endless desire that knows no lack, and last, that sober intoxication that does not come from drinking too much, that is no reeking of wine but a burning for God.

From this point that fourth degree of love can be possessed forever, when God is loved alone and above all, for now we do not love ourselves except for his sake; he is himself the reward of those who love him, the eternal reward of those who love him for eternity.

Prologue to the letter that follows

I remember that some time ago I wrote a letter to the holy Carthusian brothers in which, among other matters, I discussed these same four degrees. Perhaps I said other things in it about love, much as I have talked of it here. For that reason I think it may be helpful to include it here, especially since it is easier to transcribe what I have already to hand, ready dictated, than to compose something new.

Here begins the letter on love written to the holy brothers of La Chartreuse

True and sincere charity, I say, must be said to proceed wholly from a pure heart, a good conscience, unfeigned faith, by which we love our neighbor's good as our own. For he who loves himself most, or solely, does not love the good purely, because he loves it for his sake, not for its own. And such a man cannot obey the prophet who says, "Praise the Lord, for he is good" [Ps. 118:1]. He praises the Lord perhaps because he is good to him, but not simply because he is good. Let him take note that the same prophet utters a reproach to him: "He will acknowledge you when you do him good" [Ps. 49:18].

There are some who praise God for his power, some who praise him for his goodness to them, and some who praise him simply because he is good. The first is a slave, fearful on his own account. The second is mercenary and desires profit for himself. The third is a son who honors his father. Both he who is fearful and he who is greedy act for themselves. Only he who loves like a son does not seek his own. I think this text speaks of this kind of love. "The law of the Lord is spotless. It converts souls" [Ps. 19:7], for it alone can turn the mind from love of itself and the world and direct it to God. Neither fear nor love of self can convert the soul. They change the appearance of one's deeds from time to time, but never one's character. A slave can sometimes do God's work, but because he does not do it of his own free will, he remains in his former state of hard-heartedness. The hireling can do it too, but because he does not do it for nothing, he can be convicted of being led by his own desire. Where there is self-interest there is the desire to be allowed special terms. Where that is present there is a corner, and in corners you will find rust and dirt. Let the slave, then, have his law, the very fear by which he is constrained. Let the mercenary have his greed, by which he is held back when he is enticed and tugged at by temptation. But neither of these is without spot, and they cannot convert souls. Love truly converts souls because it makes them willing.

I have called love "unspotted" because it keeps nothing for itself. For if a man holds nothing as his own, all he has belongs to God. What belongs to God cannot be unclean. Therefore love is the immaculate law of God, and it seeks not its own profit but what benefits many. It is called the law of the Lord because he himself lives by it, and also because no one can possess it except by his gift. It does not seem absurd for me to say that even God lives by the law, for I have said that the law is nothing else but love. For what preserves the supreme and ineffable unity in the blessed Trinity but love? Love is the law then, and the law of the Lord, which in some manner holds and unites the Trinity in unity in the bond of peace. But let no one think that I am taking this love as a quality or an accident. If I did, I should be saying—perish the thought—that there is something in God that is not God. But it is that divine substance that is in no way other than itself, as John says, "God is love" [1 John 4:8].

It is love indeed, then, and it is God, and it is the gift of God. And so love gives love; the substance gives rise to the accident. Where it signifies the giver, it is the name of a substance. Where it signifies the gift, it is a quality. This is the eternal law creating and governing the universe. All things were made in weight and measure and number according to this law. Nothing is left outside this law. Even the law of all is not outside this law, for the law is nothing but itself, by which even if it does not create itself, yet it rules itself.

The slave and the mercenary have a law that is not from God. One does not love God. The other loves something more than God. They have a law that is not of the Lord. And indeed each of us can make his own law, but no one can cause it to be independent of the changeless order of the eternal law. I should say that someone had made his own law when he puts his own will before the common and eternal law, wickedly wishing to imitate his Creator, so that just as God is a law unto himself, he too wants to rule himself and make his own will law. Alas! A heavy and unendurable burden lies on all the sons of Adam, bowing our necks and bending them, bringing our life to hell. "Unhappy man that I am, who will free me from the body of this death?" [Rom. 7:24], by which I am made to tremble and am almost crushed, so that, "If the Lord did not help me, my soul would soon be in hell" [Ps. 94:17].

Weighed down by this burden, groaned he who said, "Why have you set me against you? I have become a burden to myself," [Job 7:20]. Where he said "so that I have become a burden to myself" he shows that he had been his own law, and that no one but himself had brought that about. But he said, first, addressing himself to God, "Why have you set me against you?" indicating that he had not escaped the law of God.

It is the property of the everlasting and just law of God that he who is not willing to be ruled gently is ruled painfully by himself, and he who is not willing of his own free will to take up the gentle yoke and light burden of love will bear against his will the insupportable burden of his own will. And so in a wonderful and just way, the everlasting law has captured him who runs from it and set him in opposition to it, and at the same time it has kept him in subjection to it. Yet he does not remain with God in his light and rest and glory, because he is subject to force and exiled from happiness. O Lord my God, "Why do you not take away my sin, and why do you not remove my wickedness?" [Job 7:21], so that, freed from the heavy burden of my own will, I may breathe freely under the light load of love and not be coerced by slavish fear or attracted by mercenary greed, but be moved by your spirit, the spirit of freedom by which your children live and that bears witness to my spirit that I too am one of your sons, that there is the same law for us both, and that I may be myself what you are in this world. Those who do what the Apostle says—"Owe no one anything but the debt of love" [Rom. 13:8]—they are undoubtedly as God is, and in this world they are neither slaves nor hirelings, but sons.

And so the sons are not outside the law, unless perhaps someone wants to put a different interpretation on the text "The law is not made for the righteous" [1 Tim. 1:9]. But you must know that law given in a spirit of slavery by fear is different from the law of freedom given in gentleness. Children are not under fear, but they cannot survive without love.

Do you wish to hear why there is no law for those who are good? Scripture says, "You have not received the spirit of slavery again in fear" [Rom. 8:15]. Hear, then, the just man saying of himself that he is not under the law and yet not free of the law. "I have become," he says, "as if I were under the law with those who are bound by the law, although I am not outside the law of God but bound by that of Christ" [1 Cor. 9:20–21]. So it is not right to say, "The just have no law," or "The just are outside the law," but "The law is not made for the just," that is, it is not imposed on them against their will, but freely given to them when they are willing and inspired by goodness. So the Lord says beautifully, "Take my yoke upon you," as if he said, "I do not impose it on the unwilling; but you take it if you want to; otherwise you will find not rest but labor for your souls."

The law of love is good and sweet. It is not only borne lightly and easily, but it also makes bearable the laws that make men into slaves and hirelings. It does not destroy them; it fulfills them. As the Lord says, "I have not come to take away the law, but to fulfill it"

[Matt. 5:17]. It tempers the slave's law and makes the hireling's law orderly. It lightens both. For there will never be any love without fear but chaste love. There will never be love without greed unless it is kept within bounds. Therefore love fulfills the slave's law when it overflows in devotion. It fulfills the hireling's law when it sets limits to greed.

Devotion mixed with fear does not remove the fear, but purifies it. Punishment is lifted, for while law was servitude it could not function without it. Fear remains forever but a pure and filial fear. For we read that "perfect love casts out fear" [1 John 4:18]. This is to be understood to refer to the punishment that is never absent from servile fear, as I have said—by that mode of speaking by which the cause is often given for the effect.

Greed is brought to order when love overshadows it, evils are condemned, what is better is preferred to what is merely good, and the good is desired only for the sake of what is better. When by the grace of God this is fully achieved, the body is loved, and all the goods of the body for the sake of the soul, and the goods of the soul for the sake of God, and God for his own sake.

But truly, since we are carnal and born of carnal desire, it is unavoidable that our desire and love should begin with the body, and if it is rightly directed, it will then proceed by grace through certain stages until the spirit is fulfilled. For "The spiritual does not come first but the animal, and then the spiritual" [1 Cor. 15:46]. And first it is necessary for us to bear an earthly likeness before we have a heavenly likeness. In the first instance, therefore, man loves himself for himself. He is a bodily creature, and he cannot see beyond himself. But since he sees that he cannot be the author of his own existence, he begins to inquire after God by faith because he needs him, and he begins to love him. And so he comes to love God in the second degree, but still for himself and not for God's sake. But then when he begins to worship him and to keep coming to him because he needs him, God gradually begins to make himself known to him through his thinking, reading, prayer, and obedience. By this growing familiarity God causes him truly to feel his sweetness. In this way, when he has tasted how sweet the Lord is, he passes to the third stage, where he loves God not now for himself, but for God's sake. Truly he remains for a long time in that state, and I do not know whether the fourth stage, where a man comes to love himself only for God's sake, is fully attained by anyone in this life.

If anyone has experienced it, let him say so. To me it seems impossible. But I have no doubt that that is how it will be when the good and faithful servant is led into the joy of his Lord and intoxicated by the riches of the house of God. It will be as though in some miraculous way he forgets himself and, as though going out of himself altogether, comes wholly to God and afterward holds fast to him, one with him in spirit. I think this is what the prophet felt when he said, "I shall enter into the power of the Lord. Lord, I shall be mindful of your justice" [Ps. 71:16]. He knew well that when he entered into the spiritual power of the Lord, he would have cast off all the weaknesses of the flesh. He would no longer need to give it a thought. In the spirit, he would have eyes for nothing but God's justice.

Then surely the individual members of Christ [1 Cor. 6:15] can say for themselves what Paul said of their Head, "And if we have known Christ according to the flesh, we have not known him" [1 Cor. 5:16]. No one knows himself according to the flesh, for "flesh and blood will not possess the kingdom of God" [1 Cor. 15:50]. That is not because the flesh will not exist as a substance in the future, but because every need of the flesh will vanish and fleshly love will be absorbed in the love of the spirit, and the weak human affections we have now will be changed into divine affections.

Then the net of love, which ceaselessly drags every kind of fish from the great wide sea, will be drawn in to shore; the bad will be cast out, and he will keep only the good. In this life he enfolds every kind of fish within the folds of his wide-ranging love, and for the time being it wraps itself round them all, drawing all in, both those who are against him and those who are for him. Making them in some way all his own, he does not only rejoice with those who rejoice; he weeps with those who weep. But when the net is drawn to shore, all that has been suffered in sadness will be thrown out like rotten fish, and he will keep only what pleases him and is a joy.

But surely even then Paul (to take an example) will either be made weak with the weak or burn for those who are made to suffer when scandal and weakness no longer exist? Will he grieve for those who do not repent, when there is neither sinner nor penitent? Perish the thought that he should weep for those who have been condemned to eternal fire with the devil and his angels when he is in that city the rush of whose river brings joy and whose gates the Lord loves more than all the tents of Jacob. Even if there is now sometimes rejoicing in victory, yet there is strain in battle and life is in danger. Yet in that land that is home there is no more sorrow or adversity, as the song says, "Just as the dwelling place of all who rejoice is in you" [Ps.87:7], and again, "Everlasting joy will be theirs." Finally, how can mercy be remembered when the only thought is of God's justice? There will be no place for wretchedness, no time for mercy; there will then surely be no feeling of compassion.

SERMONS ON
THE SONG OF SONGS

Bernard always had a special love for The Song of Songs. Early in his monastic career, when he made himself ill by overwork, he spent some time in a hut in the monastery garden resting and convalescing. William of St. Thierry spent some time with him there, himself convalescent, and they talked of The Song of Songs so as to pass the time in a constructive way. The themes of The Song of Songs were always in his mind as he wrote and preached, and in 1135 he began a series of sermons that was to continue, with breaks when he was absent from Clairvaux, until his death in 1153.

He found matter there for reflection on current affairs, on his own personal experiences, and on human life and the love of God. It proved both a book about the present and particular and a hymn to eternal things. He points out that there must be points of likeness between self-knowledge and knowledge of God, or we could not learn from one about the other, as God clearly intends us to do (Sermon 30.1ff.).

This is a consistent emphasis in Bernard's spirituality. He preaches our value in God's eyes, but at the same time he sees that value as lying in God himself, through the union with God that the perfect among us will one day enjoy. Self-knowledge is worthwhile, but only because it will be swallowed up in the knowledge and love of God. The kiss of contemplation is a participation in the life and love of the Trinity. Human dignity consists in our capacity to return to God, to become again the beings God made.

The "likeness" is portrayed in The Song of Songs as the bond between Bridegroom and Bride. The bond holds, not by any human act but by the action of divine grace. It is a likeness that can never be finally lost. Even in exile, in the "region of unlikeness," the soul retains an inborn resemblance to God (Sermon 27.6).

> Among the sermons translated here are the opening series, on the
> "kiss" of the soul and her Bridegroom, and one of the later sermons, in
> which Bernard conveys most vividly the quality of his personal experi-
> ence of rapture in contemplation.
>
> —G. R. Evans

Sermon 2

On the Kiss

When I reflect, as I often do, on the ardor with which the patriarchs longed for the incarnation of Christ, I am pierced with sorrow and shame. And now I can scarcely contain my tears, so
ashamed am I of the lukewarmness and lethargy of the present
times. For which of us is filled with joy at the realization of this
grace as the holy men of old were moved to desire by the promise
of it?

Soon now we shall be rejoicing at the celebration of his birth.
But would that it were really for his birth! How I pray that that
burning desire and longing in the hearts of these holy men of old
may be aroused in me by these words: "Let him kiss me with the
kiss of his mouth" [Song of Sgs. 1:2]. In those days a spiritual man
could sense in the Spirit how great would be the grace released by
the touch of those lips. For that reason, speaking in the desire
prompted by the Spirit, he said, "Let him kiss me with the kiss of
his mouth," desiring with all his heart that he would not be
deprived of a share in that sweetness.

The good men of those days could say, "Of what use to me are the words the prophets have uttered? Rather, let him who is beautiful beyond the children of men kiss me with the kiss of his mouth. I am no longer content with what Moses says, for he sounds to me like someone who cannot speak well" [Exod. 4:10]. Isaiah is "a man of unclean lips" [Isa. 6:5]. Jeremiah is a child who does not know how to speak. All the prophets are empty to me.

But he, he of whom they speak, let him speak to me. Let him kiss me with the kiss of his mouth. Let him not speak to me in them or through them, for they are "a watery darkness, a dense cloud" [Ps. 18:11]. But let him kiss me with the kiss of his mouth, whose gracious presence and eloquence of wonderful teaching causes a "spring of living water" to well up in me to eternal life [John 4:14]. Shall I not find that a richer grace is poured out upon me from him whom the Father has anointed with the oil of gladness more than all his companions, if he will deign to kiss me with the kiss of his mouth? His living and effective word is a kiss; not a meeting of lips, which can sometimes be deceptive about the state of the heart, but a full infusion of joys, a revelation of secrets, a wonderful and inseparable mingling of the light from above and the mind on which it is shed, which, when it is joined with God, is one spirit with him.

It is with good reason, then, that I have nothing to do with dreams and visions and reject figures and mysteries; even the beauty of angels seems tedious to me. For my Jesus outshines them so far in his beauty and loveliness. That is why I ask him, not any other, angel or man, to kiss me with the kiss of his mouth.

I do not presume to think that I shall be kissed by his mouth. That is the unique felicity and singular prerogative of the humanity he assumed. But, more humbly, I ask to be kissed by the kiss of his mouth, which is shared by many, those who can say, "Indeed, from his fullness we have all received" [John 1:16].

Listen carefully here. The mouth that kisses signifies the Word who assumes human nature; the flesh that is assumed is the recipient of the kiss; the kiss, which is of both giver and receiver, is the Person who is of both, the Mediator between God and man, the man Christ Jesus. For this reason, none of the saints presumed to say, "Let him kiss me with his mouth," but "with the kiss of his mouth," thus acknowledging that prerogative of him on whom uniquely once and for all the Mouth of the Word was pressed, when the whole fullness of the divinity gave itself to him in the body.

O happy kiss, and wonder of amazing self-humbling, which is not a mere meeting of lips, but the union of God with man. The touch of lips signifies the bringing together of souls. But this conjoining of natures unites the human with the divine and makes peace between earth and heaven. "For he himself is our peace, who made the two one" [Eph. 2:14]. This was the kiss for which the holy men of old longed, the more so because they foresaw the joy and exultation of finding their treasure in him and discovering all the treasures of wisdom and knowledge in him, and they longed to receive of his fullness.

I think that what I have said pleases you. But listen to another meaning.

The holy men who lived before the coming of the Savior understood that God had in mind a plan to bring peace to the race of mortal men. For the Word would do nothing on earth that he did not reveal to his servants the prophets. But this Word was hidden from many, for at that time faith was rare upon the earth and hope was very faint, even in the hearts of many of those who were waiting for the redemption of Israel. Those who foreknew also proclaimed that Christ would come in the flesh and that with him would come peace. That is why one of them says, "There will be peace when he comes to our earth." By divine inspiration they preached faithfully that men were to be saved through the grace of God. John, the forerunner of the Lord, recognized that this was to be fulfilled in his own time, and he declared, "Grace and truth have come through Jesus Christ" [John 1:17], and all Christian peoples now experience the truth of what he said.

In those days, although the prophets foretold peace, the faith of the people continually wavered because there was no one to redeem or save them, for the Author of peace delayed his coming. So men complained at the delay, because the Prince of Peace, who had been so often proclaimed, had not yet come, as had been promised by the holy men who were his prophets from of old.

They began to lose faith in the promises, and they demanded the kiss, the sign of the promise of reconciliation. It was as if one of the people were to answer the messengers of peace, "How much longer are you going to keep us waiting?" [John 10:24]. You foretell a peace that does not come. You promise good things, and there is still confusion. See, many times and in many ways angels announced to the patriarchs and our fathers proclaimed to us, saying, "Peace. And there is no peace" [Jer. 6:14]. If God wants me to believe in his benevolent will, which he has so often spoken of through the prophets but not yet shown in action, "Let him kiss me with the kiss of his mouth," and so by this sign of peace make peace secure. For how am I to go on believing in mere words? They need to be confirmed by deeds. Let him confirm that his messengers spoke the truth, if they were his messengers, and let him follow them in person, as they have so often promised; for they can do nothing without him. He sent a boy bearing a staff, but no voice or life.

I do not rise up or awaken; I am not shaken free of the dust; I do not breathe in hope, if the prophet himself does not come down and kiss me with the kiss of his mouth.

Here we must add that he who makes himself our Mediator with God is the Son of God and he is himself God. What is man that he should take notice of him, or the son of man, that he should think of him [Ps. 144:3]? Where am I to find the faith to dare to trust in such majesty? How, I say, shall I, who am dust and ashes, presume to think that God cares about me? He loves his Father. He does not need me or my possessions. How then shall I be sure that he will never fail me?

If it is true, as you prophets say, that God has the intention of showing mercy, and thinks to make himself manifest for our reassurance, let him make a covenant of peace, an everlasting covenant with me by the kiss of his mouth.

If he is not going to go back on what he has said, let him empty himself, humble himself, bend low, and "kiss me with the kiss of his mouth." If the Mediator is to be acceptable to both sides, let

God the Son of God become man; let him become the son of man, and make me sure of him with the kiss of his mouth. When I know that the Mediator who is the Son of God is mine, then I shall accept him trustingly. Then there can be no mistrust. For he is brother to my flesh. For I think that bone of my bone and flesh of my flesh cannot spurn me.

So, therefore, the old complaint went on about this most sacred kiss, that is, the mystery of the incarnation of the Word, while faith faints with weariness because of its long and troubled waiting, and the faithless people murmured against the promises of God because they were worn out by waiting. Am I making this up? Do you not recognize that this is what Scripture says, "Here are complaints and the loud murmur of voices, order on order, waiting on waiting, a little here, a little there" [Isa. 28:10]? Here are anxious prayers full of piety: "Give their reward, Lord, to those who wait on you, so that your prophets may be found faithful" [Sir. 36:21]. Again, "Bring about what the prophets of old prophesied in your name" [Sir. 36:20]. Here are sweet promises full of consolation: "Behold the Lord will appear; and he will not lie. If he seems slow, wait for him, for he will come, and that soon" [Heb. 2:3]. Again, "The time of his coming is near, and his days will not be prolonged" [Isa. 13:22], and, from the Person of him who was promised, "Behold," he says, "I am running toward you like a river of peace, and like a stream in flood with the glory of the nations" [Isa. 66:12].

In these words, both the urgency of the preachers and the lack of faith of the people are clear enough. And so the people murmured and faith wavered and, as Isaiah puts it, "The messengers of peace weep bitterly" [Isa. 33:7]. Therefore, because Christ delayed

his coming lest the whole human race should perish in desperation while they thought their weak mortality condemned them
and they did not trust that God would bring them the so often
promised reconciliation with him, those holy men who were
made sure by the Spirit looked for the certainty that his presence
could bring, and urgently demanded a sign that the covenant was
about to be renewed for the sake of the weak in the faith.

O Root of Jesse, who stand as a sign to the peoples, how many
kings and prophets wanted to see you and did not? Simeon is the
happiest of them all because by God's mercy he was still bearing
fruit in old age. For he rejoiced to think that he would see the sign
so long desired. He saw it and was glad. When he had received the
kiss of peace he departed in peace, but first he proclaimed aloud
that Jesus was born, a sign that would be rejected.

And so it was. The sign of peace arose and was rejected by those
who hate peace. For what is peace to men of goodwill is a stone to
make men stumble, a rock for the wicked to fall over. "Herod was
troubled, and all Jerusalem with him" [Matt. 2:3]. He came to his
own and his own did not receive him. Happy those shepherds
keeping watch at night who were found worthy to be shown the
sign of this vision. For even at that time he was hiding himself
from the wise and prudent and revealing himself to the simple.
Herod wanted to see him, but because he did not want to see him
out of goodwill, he did not deserve to see him.

The sign of peace was given only to men of goodwill; the only
sign given to Herod and his like is the sign of Jonah and the
prophet. The angel said to the shepherds, "This is a sign for you"
[Luke 2:12], you who are humble, you who are obedient, you

who are not haughty, you who are keeping vigil and meditating on God's law day and night. "This is a sign for you," he said.

What is this sign? The sign the angels promised, the sign the people asked for, the sign the prophets foretold the Lord Jesus has now made, and he shows it to you; the sign in which unbelievers receive the faith, the faint-hearted hope, the perfect security. This is your sign.

What is it a sign of? Indulgence, grace, peace, the peace that will have no end. It is this sign: "You will find a baby wrapped in swaddling clothes and lying in a manger" [Luke 2:12]. But this baby is God himself, reconciling the world to himself in him. He will die for your sins and rise again to make you just, so that, made just by faith, you may be at peace with God.

This was the sign of faith that the prophet once asked Ahaz the king to ask of the Lord his God, either from the heavens or from the depths of hell. But the wicked king refused, not believing, wretched man, that in this sign the heights would be joined to the depths in peace. This came to pass when the Lord descended even to hell and greeted those who dwell there with a holy kiss, so that even they received the sign of peace, and then he returned to heaven and made it possible for the spirits there to share the same sign in everlasting joy.

We must come to the end of this sermon. But let me sum up briefly what I have said. It seems clear that this holy kiss was given to the world for two reasons: to give the weak faith and to satisfy the desire of the perfect. This kiss is no other than the Mediator between God and men, the man Christ Jesus, who with the Father and the Holy Spirit lives and reigns world without end, Amen.

Sermon 3

Today we read the book of experience. Let us turn to ourselves and let each of us search his own conscience about what is said. I want to investigate whether it has been given to any of you to say, "Let him kiss me with the kiss of his mouth" [Song of Sgs. 1:2]. Few can say this wholeheartedly. But if anyone once receives the spiritual kiss of Christ's mouth, he seeks eagerly to have it again and again. I think no one can know what it is except he who has received it. It is a hidden manna, and he who eats it hungers for more. It is a sealed-up fountain, to which no stranger has access, but he who drinks from it thirsts for more, and he alone.

Hear the demand of one who has experienced it: "Restore to me the joy of your salvation" [Ps. 51:12]. But a soul like mine, burdened with sins, cannot dare to say that while it is still crippled by fleshly passions, does not feel the sweetness of the Spirit, and is almost wholly unfamiliar with and inexperienced in inner joys.

But I should like to point out to the man who is like this that there is a place for him on the road to salvation. He may not rashly lift his face to the face of the most serene Bridegroom, but he can throw himself timidly at the feet of the most severe Lord with me, and with the publican tremble on the earth and not look up to heaven, in case he is dazzled by the light. Eyes that are used to darkness will be blinded by light and wrapped again in a darkness deeper than before. You who are such a soul do not think that position despicable in which the sinner laid down her sins and put on the garment of holiness. There the Ethiopian changed her skin and, restored to a new brightness, she could reply faithfully and truthfully to those who reproached her, "I am black but I am beautiful, daughters of Jerusalem" [Song of Sgs. 1:5].

Are you wondering how she was able to change like this, or how she deserved it? You shall hear in a few words. She wept bitterly and sighed deeply from her inmost heart, and her sobs shook her one by one, and the evils within her came forth. The heavenly Physician came quickly to help her, for "his Word runs swiftly" [Ps. 147:15].

Surely the Word of God is not a medicine? Indeed it is, strong and powerful, searching out the heart and mind. "God's word is living and effective, and more penetrating than any two-edged sword, penetrating to the place where soul and spirit meet, and separating the marrow; it judges the thoughts" [Heb. 4:12].

O wretch, prostrate yourself like this blessed penitent, so that you can cease to be miserable. Prostrate yourself on the ground, embrace his feet, plead with kisses, water them with tears. Wash not only him but yourself, and you will become one of the flock of shorn ewes as they come up from the washing. Even then you will not dare to lift your face, swollen with shame and grief, until you hear him say, "Your sins are forgiven" [Luke 7:48], and "Awake, awake captive daughter of Zion, awake, shake off the dust" [Isa. 52:1–2].

Though you have given a first kiss to the feet, do not presume to rise at once to kiss the mouth. You must come to that by way of another, intermediate kiss, on the hand. This is the reason for that kiss: "If Jesus says to me, 'Your sins are forgiven,' what is the good of that unless I cease to sin? I have taken off my filthy garment. If I put it on again, what progress have I made?" [Song of Sgs. 5:3]. If I dirty again the feet that I have washed, surely the washing is value-less? Filthy with every sort of vice, I have lain for a long time in the slough of the mire. If I return to it again, it is worse than my first falling into it. I remember that he who healed me himself said to me, "Behold you are healed; go and sin no more, lest worse befall you" [John 5:14].

It is necessary that he who gives the will to repent should add the virtue of continence, lest I should do things to repent of worse than the first. Woe is me even if I repent, if he immediately takes away the hand without which I can do nothing. Nothing, I say, because without him I cannot repent or contain my sin. For that reason I listen to Wisdom's advice: "Do not repeat yourself at your prayers" [Sir. 7:14]. I fear the Judge's reaction to the tree that did not bear good fruit. For these reasons I am not fully satisfied by the first grace, by which I repent of my sins, unless I receive the second too, so that I may bear worthy fruits of repentance and not return like a dog to his vomit.

There remains to consider what I must seek and receive before I may presume to touch higher and more sacred things. I do not want to be there all at once. I want to proceed a step at a time. The sinner's impudence displeases God as much as the penitent's mod-esty pleases him. You will please him more readily if you live within your limits and do not seek things too high for you. It is a long leap and a difficult one from the foot to the mouth, and that way of getting there is not appropriate.

How, then, should you go? Should you who were recently cov-ered in filth touch the holy lips? Yesterday dragged out of the mire, do you present yourself today to the face of glory? Let your way be by the hand. The hand first touched you and now lifts you up. How will it lift you up? By giving you the grace to aspire. What is that? The sweetness of temperance and the fruits of worthy repentance, which are the works of holiness; these can lift you from the mire to the hope of daring greater things. When you receive this grace, you kiss his hand. Give the glory not to yourself but to him. Give it once and again, both for the forgiveness of sins and for the virtues that are given. Otherwise you will need to fortify yourself against such darts as these: "What do you have that you have not received? If you have received, why do you glory as though you had not?" [1 Cor. 4:7].

Now at last, having the experience of the divine kindness in these two kisses, perhaps you will not feel diffident of presuming to what is holier. The more you grow in grace, the more you are enlarged in faith. Thus it is that you will love more ardently and press more confidently for what you know you still lack. For, "To him who knocks it shall be opened" [Luke 11:10]. I believe that that supreme kiss of the highest condescension and wonderful sweetness will not be denied to him who so loves.

This is the way; this is the order. First we cast ourselves at his feet and deplore before God, who made us, the evil we have done. Second, we reach out for the hand that will lift us up, that will strengthen our trembling knees. Last, when we have obtained that, with many prayers and tears, then perhaps we shall dare to lift our faces to the mouth that is so divinely beautiful, fearing and trembling, not only to gaze on it, but even to kiss it. For "Christ the Lord is a Spirit before our face" [Lam. 4:20]. When we are joined with him in a holy kiss, we are made one with him in spirit through his kindness.

My heart rightly says to you, Lord Jesus, "My face has sought you; your face, Lord, do I seek" [Ps. 27:8]. In the morning you showed me your mercy. When I lay in the dust to kiss your footprints, you forgave my evil life. Later in the day you gave joy to your servant's soul, when, with the kiss of your hand, you gave him grace to live a good life. And now what remains, O good Lord, except that now in full light, while I am in fervor of spirit, you should admit me to the kiss of your mouth and grant me the full joy of your presence. Show me, O sweetest and most serene, "Show me where you feed, where you lie down in the noonday" [Song of Sgs. 1:7].

Brothers, it is good for us to be here, but the duties of the day call us away. These guests whose arrival has just been announced to us oblige me to break off my sermon rather than bring it to an end. So I am going to our guests, so as not to neglect the duty of charity of which we have been speaking—lest we hear it said of us, "They do not practice what they preach" [Matt. 23:3]. In the meantime, pray that the words of my mouth may be pleasing to God, for your edification and for his praise and glory.

Sermon 4

Yesterday's sermon outlined the progression of the soul in three stages by means of the image of three kisses. You have not forgotten? Today, I shall continue the argument, as far as God in his goodness may allow his poor one. We said, if you remember, that those kisses are given to the feet, the hands, the mouth, one after the other. The first comes at the beginning of our Christian life. The second is given to those who are making progress. The third is a rare experience, given only to the perfect.

The Scripture we are trying to expound begins from this last alone, and we have added the other two for its sake. Whether it was necessary you shall judge. For I think that the way the word is presented requires it. It would be surprising if you did not see that there was something else, other kisses, which she who said "he kisses me with the kiss of his mouth" [Song of Sgs. 1:2] wanted to distinguish from the kiss of the mouth. Why, then, when she could have said simply "he kisses me," did she distinctly and pointedly add, contrary to ordinary usage, "with the kiss of his mouth," unless it was to show that the supreme kiss she wanted was not the only one?

Surely we say in her place, "Kiss me" or "give me a kiss"? No one adds, "with your mouth" or "with the kiss of your mouth." What? When we are going to kiss one another, we do not have to say what we want when we offer our lips to one another. To take an example: St. John simply says when he describes the kiss that Judas gave the Lord, "And he kissed him." He does not add "with his mouth" or "with the kiss of his mouth." So with everyone who speaks or writes.

There are, then, these three affections or stages of progress in the soul. They are well enough known and obvious to those who have experienced them. First there is the forgiveness of sins; then the grace to do good; then the presence of him who forgives, the benefactor, is experienced as strongly as it can be in a fragile body.

Hear why I called the first and second stages "kisses." We all know that a kiss is a sign of peace. If, as Scripture says, "our sins separate us from God" [Isa. 59:2], peace is lost between us. When, therefore, we make satisfaction and are reconciled with the removal of the sin that was separating us, the favor we receive can surely only be called a kiss. And then there is no better place for receiving this kiss than the feet. The satisfaction we make for our sins of pride ought to be humble and lowly.

But when God grants us the grace of a sweet familiarity with him, so that we can live better lives in accordance with that relationship, we lift our heads from the dust with greater confidence, so as to kiss the hand of our benefactor, as people do. But in receiving this gift we seek not our own glory but that of the giver, and we ascribe his gifts to him and not to ourselves. Otherwise, if you glory in yourself and not in the Lord, you will be kissing your own hand, not his. That, Job says, is the great sin and a denial of God. If, then, Scripture bears witness that to seek one's own glory is to kiss one's own hand, then he who gives the glory to God is not improperly said to kiss God's hand. We see that this is even among men. Slaves kiss the feet of the masters they have offended when they ask their pardon, and the poor kiss the hands of the rich when they receive gifts from them.

Truly, since "God is a Spirit" [John 4:24], his simple substance cannot have bodily members. Perhaps you will not accept all this, but demand that I show you these hands and feet of God and so support what I say about the kiss of the feet and the hands.

But what if I, in my turn, ask about the mouth of God, for Scripture certainly speaks of the kiss of a mouth? Show me how God has a mouth. Either he has a mouth, hands, and feet, or he has none of these things. But God has a mouth by which he teaches men knowledge, and a hand by which he gives food to all flesh, and he has feet, for which the earth is a footstool. When the sinners of the earth turn from their sins and are humbled, it is to these feet that they come with a kiss.

God has all these not by nature, but we understand them as ways by which we can come to him. A truly humble desire to confess casts us down before him as if at his feet. A burning devotion to God discovers renewal and refreshment in him as at the touch of his hand. A joyous contemplation finds rest in him in the rapture that is the kiss of his mouth.

He who governs all is all things to all, yet he has no particularities. All that we can say of him in himself is that "he dwells in inaccessible light" [1 Tim. 6:16]. His peace is beyond our understanding. His wisdom is beyond measure, and his greatness has no bounds. No man can see him and live.

Yet he who is the ground of all being is not far from each of us, for without him is nothing. But, to make you wonder more: Nothing is more present than he, and nothing is more incomprehensible. What is more present to anyone than his own being? And what is more incomprehensible than the Being of all things? I say that God is the Being of all things not because they are the same as him, but because "from him and through him and in him are all things" [Rom. 11:36]. He is, as their Creator, the Being of all things that are made. But he is the cause, not the stuff of their being. In this way, this majesty has deigned to be present to his creatures, to be all in all things to all living things throughout their life; to all rational creatures the light of understanding; virtue to those who use their reason rightly; glory to those who conquer.

In all this creating, governing, administration, moving and causing motion, renewing and strengthening, he needs no bodily instruments, for by his word alone he created all bodies and spirits. Souls need bodies, and bodies needed senses by which to know and affect one another. But the Omnipotent is not like that. By the swift action of his will he chose to create and ordain things. He can do what he will, as much as he wills, and without the help of any bodily members. Do you think he needs the help of bodily senses to understand what he has created? Nothing at all can hide from him or flees the light of his presence. Sense awareness can never be the vehicle of his knowledge. Not only does he know all things without a body; he also causes the pure in heart to know him in this way.

I have said a good deal about this, so as to make it clear. But perhaps now that I must stop for today, we should postpone more discussion until tomorrow.

Sermon 7

I see that when I invited your questions I brought a good deal of work on myself! I tried to explain about the spiritual feet of God, with their descriptions and their names, under the heading of the first kiss. You are now asking about the hand to which the second kiss is given. I give in; I will do what you ask. I will also show you not the hand, but both hands, and give them their names. One is called "generosity" because it gives freely. The other is called "strength" because it powerfully defends what it has given. He who is not ungrateful will kiss both, in gratitude to God who is the Giver of all good things, recognizing and trusting him as Protector.

I think enough has been said about the first two kisses. Let us examine the third. "Let him kiss me," she says, "with the kiss of his mouth" [Song of Sgs. 1:2]. Who is speaking? The Bride. But why "Bride"? She is the soul that thirsts for God. I set out the different affections so as to make it clearer which properly belongs to the Bride. If someone is a slave, he fears his master's face. If he is a hireling, he hopes for payment from his master's hand. If he is a pupil, he bends his ear to his master. If he is a son, he honors his father. But she who asks for a kiss feels love. This affection of love excels among the gifts of nature, especially when it returns to its source, which is God. For no names can be found as sweet as those in which the Word and the soul exchange affections, as Bridegroom and Bride, for to such everything is common, nothing is the property of one and not the other, nothing is held separately. They share one inheritance, one table, one house, one bed, one flesh. For this she leaves her father and her mother and clings to her husband, and they two are one flesh. She is also commanded to forget her people and her father's house so that he may desire her beauty.

So then love especially and chiefly belongs to those who are married, and it is not inappropriate to call the loving soul a Bride. For she who asks a kiss feels love. She does not ask for freedom or payment or an inheritance or learning, but for a kiss, in the manner of a most chaste bride, who sighs for holy love; and she cannot disguise the flame, which is so evident.

It is a great thing she will ask of the Great One, but she does not flirt with him as others do, and she does not beat about the bush. She tells him clearly what she desires. She uses no preliminaries. She does not try to win him around. But with an open face she bursts out suddenly from a full heart: "Let him kiss me," she says, "with the kiss of his mouth." Surely it seems to you as though she said, "Who have I in heaven but you, and who but you do I want upon earth?" [Ps. 73:25].

She loves most chastely who seeks him whom she loves and not some other thing that belongs to him. She loves in a holy way, because she does not love in fleshly desire, but in purity of spirit. She loves ardently, because she is drunk with love so that she cannot see his majesty. What? He it is "who looks on the earth and causes it to tremble" [Ps. 104:32]. And she asks him for a kiss? Is she drunk? Indeed she is! And perhaps then when she burst forth thus she had come out of the wine cellar. She said afterward that she had been there, glorying in it. For David too said to God concerning such, "They shall be intoxicated with the plenty of your house, and you will give them the torrents of your pleasure to drink" [Ps. 36:8]. Oh, what force of love! What great confidence of spirit! What freedom! What is more evident than that perfect love casts out fear?

But modestly she does not speak directly to the Bridegroom himself, but to others, as if he were not present. "Let him kiss me," she says, "with the kiss of his mouth." She asks a great thing, and it is necessary that such prayer should be accompanied by modesty, to commend the request. And so through servants and intimates one seeks to be allowed to enter a house and reach one's desire.

Who are these? We believe that the angels stand by in prayer, to offer God the prayers and vows of men, where they can see that the prayer is offered with clean hands upraised, without anger or deceit. The angel speaking to Tobias demonstrates it: "When you prayed with tears and buried your dead and left your table and hid the dead by day in your house for burial at night, I bore your prayer to the Lord" [Tob. 12:12]. I think you are sufficiently persuaded by this and other testimonies of Scripture. For the Psalmist shows clearly that the holy angels are accustomed to mingle their songs with ours. "The princes went before with the singers in the midst of young damsels playing the timbrels" [Ps. 68:25]. He also said, "I will sing praise to you in the sight of the angels" [Ps. 138:1].

I grieve to find some of you deep in sleep during the night office; showing no respect for the criticisms of heaven, you appear before these princes like dead men; yet they are deeply moved when you show eagerness, and they delight to be present at your solemn services. I fear that sometimes they may be horrified by our casualness and go away indignantly, and then when it is too late each of us will begin to groan aloud and say to God, "You have put my friends far from me; they have found me an abomination" [Ps. 88:8]. Or, "You have turned my friend and my neighbor against me; those who know me will not share my misery" [Ps. 88:18]. Again, "Those who were close to me stand far off, and those who sought my soul were violent" [Ps. 38:11ff.].

If the good spirits stand far away from us, who will bear the attack of the wicked? I say, then, to those who behave in this way, "Cursed is he who does the work of God negligently" [Jer. 48:10]. He says too, not I but the Lord, "Would that I found you hot or cold. But because I find you lukewarm, I spit you out of my mouth" [Rev. 3:15–16ff.]. For that reason, think of these princes when you stand up to pray or sing; stand with reverence and discipline, and glory that your angels daily see the Father's face. Sent to serve for our sake, who are heirs of salvation, they carry our devotion to the heights and bring us grace in return. Let us make use of their help, we who share their destiny, so that praise may be made perfect by the mouths of babes in arms. Let us say to them, "Sing praises to God, sing praises." And let us hear them responding in turn, "Sing praises to our King, sing praises" [Ps. 47:6].

Singing praises, then, with the heavenly singers, sing wisely, as fellow citizens with the saints and members of God's household. Food tastes sweet in the mouth, a psalm in the heart. But the faithful and wise soul will not neglect to tear at the psalm with the teeth of its understanding. If you swallow it whole without chewing it, the palate will miss the delicious flavor that is sweeter than honey from the honeycomb. Let us with the apostles offer the honeycomb in the heavenly banquet at the Lord's table. The honey in the wax is the devotion in the words. Otherwise, the letter kills if you eat it without the condiment of the spiritual meaning. But if, with the Apostle, you sing with the spirit and with the mind too, you will know as he did the truth of Jesus' saying, "The words I have spoken to you are spirit and life" [John 6:64], and also, "My spirit is sweeter than honey" [Sir. 24:20].

In this way your soul will be delighted in fatness; in this way your sacrifice will be full of richness. In this way you will please the king, if you please the princes and make all his court well disposed toward you. And when they smell this sweet scent in heaven, they will say of you too, "Who is this who comes up from the desert like a column of smoke, fragrant with myrrh and frankincense and with all the spices of the merchant?" [Song of Sgs. 3:6].

"The princes of Judah," says the Psalmist, "are their leaders, the princes of Zebulun, the princes of Naphtali" [Ps. 68:27], the angelic leaders of the faithful, the continent, those in contemplation. These princes know how acceptable to our king is the confession of those who sing psalms, the fortitude of the continent, the purity of those in contemplation. And they are anxious to make us show those firstfruits of the spirit that are nothing but the first and purest fruits of wisdom. For you know that in Hebrew Judah means someone who praises or makes acknowledgment, Zebulun a fortified dwelling, Naphtali a swift hind, which by its agile leaps signifies the ecstasies of the soul in contemplation. The hind also finds its way into the dark woods, as the contemplative soul sees into the hidden meanings of things. We know who said, "The sacrifice of praise honors me" [Ps. 50:23].

If, truly, "praise is ugly in a sinner's mouth" [Sir. 15:9], you will see how absolutely necessary is the virtue of continence, through which sin is prevented from ruling in your mortal body. But continence will gain you no merit before God if you practice it to win glory among men. And so the most important thing is purity of intention, by which your mind seeks to please only God and is able to cling to him. For to "cling to" God is nothing but to see God, and that is given as a special happiness only to the pure in heart. David had a pure heart. He said to God, "My soul clings to you" [Ps. 63:8], and again, "My joy lies in being near to God" [Ps. 73:28]. By his vision, he clung to him; by clinging he beheld him.

Souls exercised in these heavenly ways show themselves to be intimates of the angels and fellow members of their family, especially if the angels often come upon him in prayer. Who will grant, O kind princes, that my petitions may be made known before God? It is not that they need to be made known to God, who knows all the thoughts of men, but before God, that is, to those who are with God, the blessed virtues and those souls that are separated from their bodies.

Who will raise me up in my poverty from the earth and lift this poor man from the dunghill, that I may be seated with the princes and be given a seat in glory? I do not doubt that they will gladly welcome into their mansions him whom they did not disdain to visit on the dunghill. And if our conversation pleased them, will they not welcome us when we join them?

And so I think that it was to these, her companions and members of her household, that the Bride spoke when she opened up her heart and said, "Let him kiss me with the kiss of his mouth." See the familiar and friendly conversation that the longing soul still in the body has with the heavenly powers. She desires to be kissed, and she asks for what she desires. But she does not name him whom she loves, because she has so often spoken of him to them. Therefore she does not say, "Let him, or him, kiss me," but just, "Let him kiss me," just as Mary Magdalene did not say the name of him whom she sought, but she spoke to the man she thought was the gardener, "Lord, if you have taken him away . . . " [John 20:15]. Who is "him"? She does not say. She takes it for granted that everyone knows who it is, who is never for a moment out of her thoughts. And so then she, speaking to the Bridegroom's companions, takes it that they know what she means, and she speaks no name when she bursts forth about her beloved: "Let him kiss me with the kiss of his mouth."

I do not want to keep you longer today to talk of the kiss, but in tomorrow's sermon you will hear from me whatever your prayers can draw from him whose teaching is the source of all we know. For flesh and blood do not reveal such a secret, but only he who sees into the depths of God, the Holy Spirit, who, proceeding from the Father and the Son, lives and reigns equally with them forever.

Sermon 8

You will remember that yesterday I promised that I would speak today about the supreme kiss, the kiss of the mouth. Listen the more carefully to what tastes the sweeter, is enjoyed the more rarely, and is the more difficult to understand.

I think I should begin by speaking briefly about that highest kiss that is beyond description and that no creature has experienced, the kiss that was referred to in these words: "No one has known the Son except the Father, and no one has known the Father except the Son or him to whom the Son has chosen to reveal him" [Matt. 11:27]. For the Father loves the Son and embraces him with a special love. He who is supreme embraces his equal; he who is eternal embraces him who is eternal; the One embraces his only Son. But the Son is bound to him by no less a bond. For his love he even dies, as he himself bears witness when he says, "So that all may know that I love the Father, rise, let us go" [John 14:31]. He went, as we know, to his Passion. And so that mutual love and knowledge between him who begets and him who is begotten, what is it but that sweetest and most mysterious kiss?

I myself am sure that no creature, not even an angel, is admitted to such and so holy a secret of divine love. Does not Paul say from his own knowledge that that peace surpasses all understanding, even that of the angels? That is why the Bride, although she is bold in many things, does not dare to say, "Let him kiss me with his mouth," for that is reserved for the Father alone. But she asks something less. "Let him kiss me," she says, "with the kiss of his mouth." See the new Bride receiving the new kiss, not from the Bridegroom's mouth but from the kiss of his mouth.

"He breathed on them," it says, and that certainly means that Jesus breathed on the apostles, that is, the primitive Church, and said, "Receive the Holy Spirit" [John 20:22]. That was the kiss. What was it? A breath? No, but the invisible Spirit, who is so bestowed in the breath of the Lord that he is understood to have proceeded from the Son as well as from the Father.

The kiss is truly common to him who kisses and to him who is kissed. And so it satisfies the Bride to receive the Bridegroom's kiss, although it is not a kiss from his mouth. For she thinks it not a small or light thing to be kissed by the kiss, for that is nothing but to be given the Holy Spirit. Surely if the Father kisses and the Son receives the kiss, it is appropriate to think of the Holy Spirit as the kiss, for he is the imperturbable peace of the Father and the Son, their secure bond, their undivided love, their indivisible unity.

It is he who prompts the Bride's boldness, and it is he whom she trustingly asks to come to her when she asks for a kiss. She has a reason to be bold, which never fails. For the Son, when he said, "No one has known the Son except the Father, and no one has known the Father except the Son," added, "or him to whom the Son has chosen to reveal him" [Matt. 11:27]. The Bride has no doubt that if he is willing to reveal him to anyone, it is to her. Therefore she asks boldly to be given the kiss, that is, the Spirit in whom the Father and the Son will reveal themselves to her. For one of them cannot be known without the other. That is why Christ said, "He who has seen me has also seen the Father" [John 14:9]. And John, "He who denies the Son does not have the Father. He who believes in the Son has the Father too" [1 John 2:23].

From this it is clear that the Father is not known without the Son, and the Son is not known without the Father. The supreme happiness consists in the knowledge not of one but of both, as, "This is everlasting life, to know that you are the true God and to know Jesus Christ whom you have sent" [John 17:3]. So those who follow the Lamb are said to have his name and that of the Father written on their foreheads, and that is to be glorified by the knowledge of both.

But someone is saying, "Therefore it is not necessary to know the Holy Spirit, for when he said that eternal life is to have known the Father and the Son, he made no mention of the Holy Spirit." That is so, but where Father and Son are known fully, how can their goodness, which is the Holy Spirit, not be known? For no man really knows another as long as he does not know whether he is a man of goodwill or not. So although it has been said, "This is everlasting life, to know that you are the true God and to know Jesus Christ, whom you have sent" [John 17:3], that sending shows the good pleasure both of the Father, who kindly sends, and of the Son, who willingly obeys; there is an implied reference to the Holy Spirit where mention is made of such grace on the part of both. For the Holy Spirit is the love and goodness of both.

So when the Bride asks for a kiss, she begs to be flooded with the grace of this threefold knowledge as much as mortal flesh can bear. She asks it of the Son, for he is to reveal it to whom he wills. Therefore the Son reveals himself to whom he wills, and he reveals the Father when he does so. It is undoubtedly through the kiss that he makes this revelation, that is, through the Holy Spirit. The Apostle bears witness to this when he says, "But God revealed himself to us through his Spirit" [1 Cor. 2:10]. But in giving the Spirit through whom he reveals, he reveals him as well. In giving he reveals him; in revealing he gives him. The revelation he makes through the Holy Spirit does not only illuminate the understanding; it also fires with love, as the Apostle says, "The love of God is diffused in our hearts through the Holy Spirit that has been given us" [Rom. 5:5].

That is perhaps why we do not read that those who know God but do not give him glory do not know him through the revelation of the Holy Spirit, for although they know him, they do not love him. Thus you have, "God has revealed himself to them" [Rom. 1:19], but Paul does not add, "through the Holy Spirit," lest those wicked minds should think themselves to have received the kiss of the Bride. They were content with a knowledge that puffed them up, but they did not know about that which builds up. The Apostle tells us how they knew. "They perceived him in the things he had made" [Rom. 1:20].

It is clear from this that they did not fully know him, for they did not love him. For if they had fully known him, they could not have been ignorant of the goodness that made him willing to be born and to die for their redemption. Hear what was revealed to them about God, "his everlasting power and divinity" [Rom. 1:20]. You see that in their presumption of spirit (their own spirit, not the Spirit of God) they considered his sublimity and majesty, but they did not understand that he was meek and lowly of heart. That is not surprising, for their leader Behemoth sees everything that is high, nothing that is humble. But David did not walk in great things, nor in wonders above himself. He was not a peerer into majesty, in case he should be dazzled by glory.

You too always remember the words of the wise, so that you may be cautious in stepping into mysteries. "Do not try to understand things that are too difficult for you, or try to discover what is beyond your powers" [Sir. 3:21]. Walk in such things in the Spirit and not by your own senses. The teaching of the Spirit does not sharpen curiosity; it inspires love. The Bride rightly, when she seeks him whom her heart loves, does not trust her senses or rely on the vain speculations of human curiosity; she asks for a kiss. That is, she calls on the Holy Spirit, through whom she will receive at the same time both the taste of knowledge and the savor of grace. And the knowledge that is given in a kiss is received with love, for a kiss is the sign of love. The knowledge that puffs up does not come from a kiss, for it is loveless. But they who have a zeal for God but not by knowing him cannot in any way lay claim to it. For the grace of the kiss brings with it a double gift, both the light of knowledge and the wealth of devotion. He is the Spirit of wisdom and understanding. Like a bee carrying both wax and honey, he has the power to kindle the light of knowledge and to pour out the savor of grace. Neither he who understands the truth without love nor he who loves without understanding, then, can think himself to have received this kiss. This kiss leaves no room for error or apathy.

Therefore let the Bride who is about to receive the twofold grace of this holy kiss prepare her two lips, her reason for the gift of understanding, her will for the gift of wisdom, so that, rejoicing in the fullness of the kiss, she may deserve to hear, "Your lips are moist with grace, for God has blessed you forever" [Ps. 45:2].

And so the Father, kissing the Son, pours into him in full the mysteries of his divinity and breathes the sweetness of love. Scripture says so when it remarks that "day to day pours forth speech" [Ps. 19:2]. As we have said, no creature has been given the privilege of witnessing this eternal unique and blessed embrace. Only the Holy Spirit is witness and able to share their mutual knowledge and love. "For who has known the mind of the Lord, or who has been his counselor?" [Rom. 11:34].

But perhaps someone will say to me, "What thunderous voice, then, told you what you say no creature knows?" I reply, "It is the only begotten Son, who is in the bosom of the Father. He has made him known" [John 1:18]. He has made him known, I say, not to me, unworthy wretch that I am, but to John, the Bridegroom's friend, for these are his words; and he made him known to John the Evangelist too, the disciple Jesus loved. For his soul was pleasing to the Lord and worthy both of the dowry and the name of a Bride, deserving the Bridegroom's embraces and worthy to recline on the Bridegroom's breast. John learned from the heart of the

Only-begotten what he had learned from his Father. Not he alone, but all those to whom the Angel of Great Counsel said, "I call you friends, for all that I have heard from my Father I have told you" [John 15:15]. Paul imbibed it, for the Gospel he preached is not of men, not did he receive it through men, but by the revelation of Jesus Christ.

All these could say happily and with truth, "The Only-begotten, who was in the bosom of the Father, he has told" us [John 1:18]. And what is that telling but a kiss? But it is the kiss of a kiss, not of the mouth. Hear about the kiss of the mouth: "I and the Father are one" [John 10:30], and again, "I am in the Father and the Father in me" [John 14:10]. This is a kiss from mouth to mouth that no creature can receive. It is a kiss of peace and love. But that love surpasses all knowledge and that peace passes all understanding. Truly what eye has not seen nor ear heard and what has not entered the mind of man God revealed to Paul through his Spirit, that is, by the kiss of his mouth. Therefore, the kiss of the mouth is the Son in the Father and the Father in the Son. As we read, "Instead of the spirit of the world we have received the Spirit that comes from God, to teach us to understand the gifts he has given us" [1 Cor. 2:12].

But let us distinguish more clearly between the two. He who receives the fullness receives the kiss of the mouth. He who receives of the fullness receives the kiss of the kiss.

Paul was great. But however high he lifted up his mouth, even to the third heaven, he could only remain at a distance from the mouth of the Most High. He must be content to stay within the limits of his nature, and since he could not reach the face of glory, he humbly asked for the kiss to be given him from above.

He who did not think it robbery to be equal with God dared to speak thus, "I and the Father are one" [John 10:30], because he was united to him as an equal and embraced him as an equal. He does not beg a kiss from below, but his mouth meets the Father's mouth directly and by a unique privilege he kisses him on the mouth. Therefore the kiss Christ receives is fullness, that of Paul a participation. Christ gloried in the kiss of the mouth, and Paul only in the kiss of the kiss.

This kiss is a joy, however, through which not only is God known, but the Father loved, who is never fully known unless he is loved. Is there not a soul among you who sometimes hears the Spirit of the Son crying in his inmost heart, "Abba, Father" [Gal. 4:6]? Let him who feels himself loved by the Father realize that he is moved by the same Spirit as the Son. Trust without reserve. Be of good courage. Know yourself to be the Father's daughter in the Spirit of the Son. Know yourself to be the Bride, or sister of the Son, for you will find both these names given to her who loves the Son. Here is a text to prove it—I need not labor the point. The Bridegroom says to her, "Come into my garden, my sister, my Bride" [Song of Sgs. 5:1]. She is a sister because she is of the one Father, a Bride because she is in one spirit with him. For if carnal marriage makes two one flesh, why should not spiritual union make two one spirit? But hear too of the Father, how lovingly he calls her "daughter" to honor her, and nevertheless invites her as his own daughter-in-law to the sweet caresses of his Son: "Hear, daughter, and see, and listen; forget your people and your father's house and the King will desire your beauty" [Ps. 45:10ff.]. See from whom this bride demands a kiss. O holy soul, be reverent, for he is the Lord your

God, who perhaps ought not to be kissed, but adored with the Father and the Holy Spirit, world without end, Amen.

Sermon 84

"All night long in my little bed I sought him whom my soul loves" [Song of Sgs. 3:1]. It is a great good to seek God; I think nothing comes before it among the good things the soul may enjoy. It is the first of its gifts and its ultimate goal. None of the virtues approaches it, and it yields place to none. What could be better when nothing has a higher place? To what could it yield place, when it is the consummation of all things? What virtue can be attributed to him who does not seek God? What limit is there for him who seeks him? "Always seek his face," it says [Ps. 105:4]. I think that, even when it has found him, the soul will not cease to seek him. God is sought not on foot, but by desire. And the happy discovery of what is desired does not end desire, but extends it. The consummation of joy does not consume desire, does it? Rather, it is oil poured on flames, which itself catches fire. Thus it is. Joy will be fulfilled. But there will be no end to desire, and so no end of seeking. Put from your mind, if you can, the absence of God as the cause of this eagerness to seek him, for he is always present, and anxiety in the search, for you cannot fail to find his abundance.

Now see why I have said this as a preliminary. It is so that every soul among you that is seeking God will know that he has gone before and sought you before you sought him. Otherwise you may turn a great good into a great evil for yourself. For from great goods can arise evils no less great, when we treat as our own the good things God gives and act as though they were not gifts, not giving God the glory. So it is that those who seem greatest because of the gifts they have received count for nothing before God because they do not give thanks for them. I am putting it mildly, using inadequate words, "great" and "little," which I know do not say exactly what I mean. I have been obscure; I will make it plain. I ought to have said "good" and "evil." For truly and undoubtedly, the best of men, if he claims the credit for his goodness, is as evil as he seemed good. This is very evil. If someone says, "Perish the thought, I know that it is by the grace of God that I am as I am" [1 Cor. 15:10], yet is eager to take even the smallest credit for the grace he has received, surely he is a robber and a thief? Let such a man hear this, "Out of your own mouth I judge you, wicked servant" [Luke 19:22]. What is more wicked than for a slave to usurp his master's glory?

"All night long in my little bed I sought him whom my soul loves" [Song of Sgs. 3:1]. The soul seeks the Word, but she has first been sought by the Word. Otherwise, once she had gone out from before his face or been cast out, her eye would not look to see good again, if the Word did not seek her. Our soul is no different from a wandering spirit that does not return if she is left to herself. Hear a fugitive and a wanderer who grieves and pleads: "I have gone astray like a lost sheep. Seek your servant" [Ps. 119:176]. O man, do you wish to return? But if it is a matter of will, why do you plead? Why do you go begging for what you have in plenty in yourself? It is clear that she wishes but cannot; she is a wandering spirit that does not return. And he who does not want to return is still farther away. If a soul wants to return and seeks to be sought, I should not say she was wholly lost and abandoned. For where does she get this will? Unless I am mistaken, it is from the visitation of the Word, who has already sought her. That seeking has not been in vain, because it has made the will active, without which there can be no return.

But it is not enough to be sought once. The weakness of the soul is great, and great is the difficulty of the return. For what if she wills? Willing is idle where there is no power to act upon it. "For the will is in me," says Paul, "but I have no power to do good" [Rom. 7:18]. What does the Psalmist whom we quoted ask? Nothing but to be sought, for he would not seek unless he was sought, and he would not seek if he had been satisfied with the seeking. So he asks more, "Seek your servant," he says, so that he who has given the will may also give the power to act, at his goodwill.

But I do not think that this passage can be speaking of such a soul, which has not yet received the second grace, willing, but not yet able to approach him whom her soul loves. For how can the words that follow apply to such a soul? She rises and goes about the city, seeking her beloved in the streets and squares, and she could not do that if she herself needed to be sought. Let her do what she can, so long as she remembers that she was first sought and first loved, and that it is because of this that she seeks and loves. And let us pray, beloved, that his mercies may quickly go before us, for we are only too poor. I do not say this of everyone. For I know that many of you walk in the love with which Christ has loved us and seek him in simplicity of heart. But there are others, I am sad to say, who have not yet given us any sign of this saving and prevenient grace, men who love themselves, not the Lord, and who seek their own good, not his.

"I have sought," she says, "him whom my soul loves" [Song of Sgs. 3:1]. This is what the kindness of him who goes before you urges you to do, he who both sought you first and loved you first. You would not be seeking him or loving him unless you had first been sought and loved. You have been forestalled not only in one blessing but in two, in love and in seeking. The love is the cause of the seeking, and the seeking is the fruit of the love; and it is its guarantee. You are loved, so that you may not think that you are sought so as to be punished; you are sought, so that you may not complain that you are loved in vain. Both these sweet gifts of love make you bold and drive diffidence away, and they persuade you to return and move you to loving response. Hence comes the zeal, the ardor, to seek him whom your soul loves, for you cannot seek unless you are sought, and now that you are sought you cannot fail to seek.

But do not forget whence you came. Now, to apply what I say to myself—for that is the safest course—is it not you, my soul, who left your first husband, with whom you were happy, and broke your faith by going after your lovers? And now that you have perhaps fornicated with them and been despised by them, do you dare, impudent and shameless, to return to him whom you proudly despised? What? Do you seek the light when you deserve to be hidden, run to your Bridegroom when you deserve blows rather than kisses? It will be surprising if you do not come face-to-face with the Judge when you expected the Bridegroom.

Happy he who hears his soul answering in these words: "I do not fear because I love, which I should not do if I were not loved.

And so this is love." She who is loved has nothing to fear. Let those who do not love be afraid. Must they not constantly fear hostility? I love, and I cannot doubt that I am loved any more than that I love. Nor can I fear his face whose love I experience. In what? In that he not only sought but loved me, and made me bold in seeking. How can I not respond to his seeking since I respond to his love? How can he be angry with me for seeking him, when he overlooked my contempt for him? He will surely not thrust away the seeker whom he sought when he despised? Kind is the Spirit of the Word, and he greets me kindly, whispering to me and coaxing me to recognize the ardor and longing of the Word, which he knows well. He sees into the mysteries of God, and knows his thoughts, thoughts of peace and not of vengeance. How can I not be roused to seek him when I have experienced his mercy and been assured of his peace?

Brothers, to understand this is to be sought by the Word; to be assured is to be found. But not all receive this Word. What shall we do for our little ones? I speak of those among us who are beginners, but not fools, for they have the beginning of wisdom and are subject to one another in the fear of Christ. How shall we bring them to believe that they may be his brides, when they do not yet perceive that this is how he deals with them? But I send them to him whom they should not fail to believe. Let them read in the book what they do not see in another's heart, and because they do not see it, do not believe. It is written in the prophets, "If a man puts away his wife and she leaves him and takes another husband, will he go back to her? Will she not be dishonored and in disgrace? You have committed fornication with many lovers. But return to me, says the Lord, and I will receive you" [Jer. 3:1]. These are the

Lord's words. You cannot disbelieve them. Let them believe what they do not know from experience, so that by their faith they may in the future have the reward of experience.

I think it has been made plain enough what it is to be sought by the Word, and that this is a need not of the Word but of the soul. It only remains to say that the soul that has experienced this knows it more fully and more happily. It remains for us in what follows to teach thirsty souls how to seek him who seeks them, or, rather, we ought to learn it from her who is spoken of in this passage as seeking him whom her soul loves, the soul's Bridegroom, Jesus Christ our Lord, who is God, blessed above all, forever.

SELECTIONS FROM HIS
LETTERS

Letter 64

About 1129 Bernard wrote to Alexander, bishop of Lincoln,
on behalf of Philip, who had become a monk at Clairvaux and
who held a benefice for whose disposition the bishop was
responsible. Philip was anxious that his family should not suffer financially as a result of his action. Bernard asks the
bishop to allow his mother to keep the house he had built for
her. He takes the opportunity to paint for the bishop a picture
of the foretaste of the heavenly Jerusalem that is to be enjoyed
at Clairvaux. Bishop Alexander (1123–47) was notorious for
his self-indulgence and injustice, and Bernard adds a personal
note of exhortation to him.

—G. R. Evans

To Alexander, Bishop of Lincoln, ca. 1129

To the honorable Lord Alexander, by the grace of God bishop of
Lincoln. Bernard, abbot of Clairvaux, wishes that he may desire
to be honored more in Christ than in the world.

Your Philip, who wanted to go to Jerusalem, has found a shortcut and arrived there sooner than he expected. He crossed this
great wide sea quickly, and with a following wind he has now
landed on the shore he was making for and has dropped anchor in
a safe harbor. Now he has his feet planted in the courts of
Jerusalem and him whom he heard of in Ephrathah he has found
in the woodland plains, and he worships him gladly in the place
where he now stands. He has entered the Holy City, and his lot is
cast as a fellow heir with those to whom it is rightly said, "Now

you are not guests and strangers, but citizens with the saints and members of God's household" [Eph. 2:19]. Going in and out with them like one of the saints, he glories with the others, saying, "Our home is in heaven" [Phil. 3:20].

He has been made not a curious spectator but a loyal inhabitant and enrolled citizen of Jerusalem; and not of this earthly Jerusalem, which has a border with Arabia at Mount Sinai and is in slavery with her children, but of the free Jerusalem, which is above and mother of us all.

And if you want to know, this is Clairvaux! Clairvaux is itself Jerusalem; it is one with the Jerusalem that is in heaven in whole-hearted devotion of the mind, in similarity of life, and in spiritual kinship. Here, as Philip promises himself, he will find rest forever. He has chosen it for his dwelling place, because here is, if not yet a clear sight of it, certainly the expectation of true peace, that peace of which it is said, "The peace of God, which surpasses all that we know" [Phil. 4:7]. He wishes to be able to enjoy with your good wishes this good of his that he has received from above. Indeed, he trusts that he has it, for he knows that you are aware of that wise saying that a wise son is his father's glory.

But he asks your fatherly kindness, and we ask it too, with him and on his behalf, to allow the arrangement he has made to continue, so that his creditors may have his prebend. He does not want to cheat anyone and be found (perish the thought!) a debtor and a breaker of promises. For the gift of a contrite heart, which he offers every day, will not be accepted as long as any brother has anything against him. He also asks that the house he himself built for his mother on church lands may be granted to his mother as long as she lives, with the land he gave with it. So much for Philip.

And now a few words for you yourself. I thought I would add something, prompted by God and perhaps inspired by him, to presume to exhort you lovingly not to take the glory of the world seriously as something that will last, and so lose that glory that will never pass away. Do not love your possessions more than yourself or for your own sake, and so lose both your possessions and yourself. Do not let the pleasure of your present prosperity hide your end from you, or endless adversity will follow. Do not let the joy of this world bring about while concealing from you, and conceal from you while bringing it about, the grief that is everlasting. Do not think death is a long way off, for it may catch you when you are not ready; and when you think life will go on and on, it may suddenly come to an end when you are in the wrong frame of mind, as it is written, "When they are saying, 'Peace and security,' then suddenly death will come, like the pains of a woman in labor, and they will not escape it" [1 Thess. 5:3].

Letter 144

In the autumn of 1137, when he would have liked to return to Clairvaux, Bernard was forced to go to Apulia to try to bring an end to the sack of the Campania by Roger of Sicily and his Saracen forces. He had been working for a long time to heal the schism that had been dividing the Church under pope and antipope and bring Western Christendom together under the papacy of Innocent II. Southern Italy and Sicily were among the last areas to be settled. He writes with longing to his brothers at Clairvaux of the pain of his exile from them and the sweetness of life among them. He asks them to pray for the pope and for a number of those who are with him in Italy: Haimeric, cardinal deacon of Santa Maria Novella and chancellor, a man who had been influential in the election of Innocent II, and the same Aimeric who asked Bernard to write his treatise "On Loving God"; Cardinal Lucas, cardinal priest of St. John and St. Paul; Cardinal Chrysogonus, cardinal deacon of St. Mary in Porticu; Cardinal Ivo, who was a former Victorine canon; and two of their own number, Bruno, who was later abbot of Chiaravalle, and Bernard's brother Gerard.

To the Brothers at Clairvaux

My soul is sorrowful until I can return to you, and it will not be comforted until I am with you again. For what consolation is there for me "in this evil time" [2 Mic. 1:5] "and in the place of my exile" [Ps. 119:19]? Surely only you in the Lord? Wherever I go the sweet thought of you never leaves me; but the sweeter the memory, the more grievous the separation. "Alas for me that my exile" is not only "prolonged," but piled up [Ps. 120:6]! And, indeed, according to the prophet, "They added to the pain of my wound" [Ps. 69:26] who separated me from you in the body for a time. There is a common exile, which is hard enough to bear, in which "as long as we are in this body we are in exile from the Lord" [2 Cor. 5:6].

To this is added the further circumstance, which makes me

almost impatient, that I am forced to live without you. It is a long tribulation and a tedious waiting, to remain so long a slave to the affairs of this empty life, to be shut up in the rottenness of the body, to be bound still by the chains of death, and not to be with Christ all this time. More: I had one remedy for all this, a gift truly given from heaven. Instead of the face of glory, which is still hidden from me, I was able to see you who are the holy temple of God. The way seemed easy to me from this temple to that glory for which the prophet sighed, saying, "I have asked one thing of the Lord, and this I require, that I may dwell in the house of the Lord all the days of my life, so that I may see the Lord's will and visit his temple" [Ps. 27:4].

What can I say? How often has that solace been kept from me! And now my heart is torn for the third time, if I reckon correctly. My children are snatched from my breast before it is time. Those whom I have "begotten" in the Gospel I am not allowed to rear. I am forced to leave my own and take care of strangers, and I do not know which hurts me more, to be taken away from the one or to be burdened with the other. Good Jesus, surely my life is not to be passed in sorrow and my years in grief? O Lord, it is better for me to die than to live but not among brothers, intimates, those who are dearest. That is sweeter, safer, and more manly, as everyone agrees. It would be an act of love to give me a period of refreshment before I go away and am no more.

If it please my Lord, let my sons be allowed to close with their own hands the eyes of him who is a kind of father to them, although he is not worthy to be called "father," so that they may see his end, console him at his death, and lift up his soul on the wings of their desire to join the company of the blessed (if you judge him worthy); let them bury this poor man's body with the bodies of the poor, and if "I have found favor in your eyes" [Gen. 18:3], grant this great desire of mine for the sake of the prayers and merits of those same brothers of mine. But "not my will but yours be done" [Luke 22:42]. I do not wish to live or to die for myself.

But since you have listened to my sorrow, you must know of my consolation, if I can be said to have any. First, all the labor and trouble I suffer is, I think, in the cause of him for whom all things live. Whether I will or not, it is necessary for me to live for him who has bought my life by laying down his own, the merciful and just judge who is able to recompense us for anything we suffer for him, on that day when the world ends. If I fight for him unwillingly, his dispensation will allow for that, and I shall be an unprofitable servant. If I fight for him willingly, that is my glory. I find some rest in that thought. Then, often he has caused my work to prosper by his heavenly grace through no merit of my own, and that grace will not be profitless in me as I have often experienced; you know something of that. But how necessary to the Church my presence is and has been I should tell you personally for your consolation, if it did not sound like boasting. But for now it is better that you should hear of it through others.

At the most pressing request of the emperor and at the pope's command and that of some of the princes and leaders of the Church, I have given way, sorrowfully and reluctantly. Weak and ill and, to tell you the truth, pale with fear of death, I am forced to go to Apulia. Pray for the peace of the Church. Pray for my safety, and that I may see you again and live and die with you. And live so that your prayer may be granted.

I have written this under pressure of time, with tears and sobs, as our dear brother Baldwin will tell you, for I dictated it to him. The Church has called him to another office and another dignity. Pray for him too as my only comfort and one in whom my spirit finds great refreshment. Pray for the Lord Pope, who has a fatherly affection for me and for all of you too. And pray for the Lord Chancellor, who is like a mother to me, and for Luke and Dom Chrysogonus, and Master Ivo, who are like our brothers. Our brothers Bruno and Gerard greet you, and they too ask for your prayers.

Letter 523

Ailred, abbot of Rievaulx (1147–67), was one of the major authors of the Cistercian order in the twelfth century. He grew up at the court of the king of Scotland, but he was English born, and he returned to England to enter the monastic life as a young man. In this letter, written at the beginning of the 1140s, Bernard is encouraging him to write the book that was later published as The Mirror of Love, *to feel it not a presumption to write it, but an act of charity. Ailred had never attended the schools of northern France where so many of his contemporaries got a university education, and Bernard reassures him that he need not regard that as a disqualification for his task. God has given him a good mind and the Holy Spirit has educated him. Ailred's books show him to have been deeply read in the Bible and the church fathers, especially Augustine. He brought to his writing, as Bernard did, a vivid personal experience of the spiritual life. His treatise "On Spiritual Friendship" makes Christian Cicero's "On Friendship", and*

everything he wrote reflects both a distinctively Ailredian and
a Cistercian spirituality.

To Ailred of Rievaulx

The greatest virtue of the saints is humility, but a humility that is real because it is discreet. True humility has nothing to do with deceit; the sacrilege of disobedience destroys it.

I have asked your brotherly love; more, I have ordered you; more, I have commanded you in the name of God, to write me a little something to help those who are entangled in grievances and who are following the narrow way of self-indulgence.

I do not condemn or reprove you for excusing yourself, but I accuse you of obstinacy. It was humility to excuse yourself. But is it humility to disobey? Is it humility not to give way? More: "It is the sin of the soothsayers to refuse, and to be stubborn is wickedness and idolatry" [1 Sam. 15:23].

But you claim that it would be too heavy a burden for your girl-ish shoulders to carry and that it would be wiser not to take it on than to fall down under the weight when you have undertaken it. What I command is indeed heavy. It is difficult. It is impossible. But that gives you no excuse. I persist in my view. I repeat my command. What will you do? Surely he in whose words you make your vow says, "Let the junior know that it is best for him, and obey, trusting in God's help." You have done as much as you ought, if not more, to excuse yourself. You have gone as far as you can. You have shown why it is impossible for you, saying you are not a learned man, indeed you are almost illiterate, that you come to the monas-tic life not from a school but from a kitchen, and that you have been leading the life of a country bumpkin among rocks and hills and laboring for your daily bread in the sweat of your brow with axe and mallet. You say that in those circumstances it is easier to learn silence than skill in speaking and that an orator's rhetoric scarcely graces a poor fisherman's clothes.

I accept your excuses very gratefully; but I am aware that they fan the flame of my desire rather than extinguish it. For knowledge gotten not from the school of some grammarian but from the school of the Holy Spirit will taste the sweeter to me. And if perhaps you have this treasure in an earthenware vessel, "so that the excellence may come from God's power and not your own" [2 Cor. 4:7], what a joyful thing, what a foretaste of the future, that you should be carried from the kitchen to the monastery. For perhaps one who has been entrusted in his time with the responsibility of providing bodily food in a royal household will be procuring spiritual food and feeding those who are hungry with the Word of God in the house of our King.

I am not put off by what you say about the steepness of the mountains, the cragginess of the rocks, or the plunging valleys, for in those days the mountains will drop sweetness and the hills will flow with milk and honey, the valleys will stand thick with corn, and honey will drip from stone and oil from the hardest rock. Christ's sheep will feed among the crags and peaks. So I think that that mallet of yours will be able to strike something from those rocks that you have not taken from the books of the masters by using your sharp wits in study, and that you will have experienced something under the shade of the trees in the heat of the day that you would never have learned in the schools.

Therefore give the glory not to yourself but to his name, who not only snatched you from the lake of wretchedness and the filth of the mire, when you were in despair, from the house of death and the cesspit, but also remembering his mercies, the merciful and compassionate Lord gave the sinner hope that he would be raised up, gave light to the blind, instructed the ignorant, and taught the inexperienced. So, then, since everyone who knows you knows that what you give is not yours, why do you blush and tremble and hesitate? Why do you refuse to give it even at the command of his voice who gave you what you have to give? Do you fear to be presumptuous or to be the envy of others? As if anyone ever wrote anything useful without being envied, or as though you could be called presumptuous when you are a monk obeying his abbot.

And so I order you in the name of Jesus Christ and in the spirit of our God, that whatever thoughts about the excellence of love, its fruits, its ordering, have come to you in your daily meditations, you will not put off writing them down, so that we can see as in a mirror what love is and how sweet it is to possess; and how great an oppression there is in greed, which is its opposite; and that outward affliction does not diminish that sweetness of love, as some think, but rather increases it; and, last, with what discretion it should be exercised. Indeed, to spare your modesty, let this letter be copied at the beginning of the book, so that whatever may displease the reader in *The Mirror of Love* (for that is the title I give it) may be blamed not upon you who obey, but upon me, who forced you to write it against your will.

Farewell in Christ, beloved brother.

ABOUT THE EDITOR

HarperCollins Spiritual Classics Series Editor Emilie Griffin has long been interested in the classics of the devotional life. She has written a number of books on spiritual formation and transformation, including *Clinging: The Experience of Prayer* and *Wilderness Time: A Guide to Spiritual Retreat*. With Richard J. Foster she coedited *Spiritual Classics: Selected Readings on the Twelve Spiritual Disciplines*. Her latest book is *Wonderful and Dark Is this Road: Discovering the Mystic Path*. She is a board member of Renovaré and leads retreats and workshops throughout the United States. She and her husband, William, live in Alexandria, Louisiana.

ABOUT VINITA HAMPTON WRIGHT

Vinita Hampton Wright is a novelist, nonfiction writer, and editor who conducts creative formation workshops at conferences and retreats around the country. She is the author of the novella *The Winter Seeking* and the novels *Velma Still Cooks in Leeway, Grace at Bender Springs*, and *Dwelling Places*, as well as numerous nonfiction titles. She and her husband, Jim, a photographer, live in Chicago.